To

Iver Franklin ?

1712 Mc Clung ?

Charleston. W. Va .

Love

Mother .

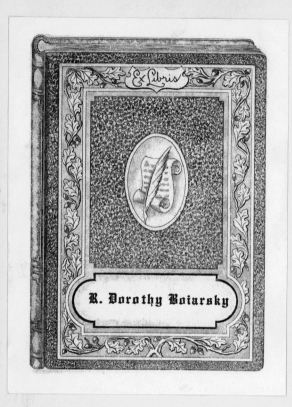

THEATRE
AT THE
LEFT

— BEN W. BROWN —

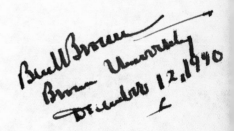

THE BOOKE SHOP
at 4 Market Square
Providence, Rhode Island

TO THE READER

BROWN UNIVERSITY generously granted me sabbatic leave to observe the scheme and methods of the state controlled theatres of Europe. The *Theatre at the Left* is an outgrowth of association with that most stimulating and progressive of subsidized stages—the theatre of the Soviet Union.

These brief essays are designed to supplement rather than rival such an excellent study as Norris Houghton's *Moscow Rehearsals*. The turbulent flux of material on the theatre of the U. S. S. R. surges with contradiction. The *Theatre at the Left* does not pretend to chart this flood with finality; it lays no claim to presenting a comprehensive or definitive exposition of the Soviet drama. It is hoped, however, that the general reader, unfamiliar with the very foreign ideals of utilitarian æsthetics, may gain from these few pages a more sympathetic understanding of this mighty and confusing movement in stagecraft and a more enthusiastic appreciation of (not necessarily a belief in) the different but idealistic standards of this *Theatre at the Left*.

My patient friends and university colleagues have my gratitude for their encouragement and help in preparing these essays. I am indebted to Anna Butrashova of Moscow and the theatre folk of the Soviet Union for opening closed doors, and especially to Alice B. Duckworth of Providence whose keen and loyal criticism has been indispensable to me.

BEN W. BROWN

Providence, Rhode Island
March 3, 1938

INTRODUCTION

AT first thought it appears strange that an economist should be asked to write a preface dealing with one of the movements in the modern theatre. But when one considers the nature of the movement, this choice on the part of the author seems quite logical.

The Russian Theatre deals with the very vitals of Russian life in its contemporary forms. It is inextricably merged with the Russian economy in two ways. In the totalitarian economy "every aspect of the life of the people" is harnessed to specific forms of organization and to given purposes. Thus the theatre is as definitely a part of the economy as the factory or the farm. *The Plan* determines the part it shall play in Russian life as a whole; its importance and its limitations, its objectives, and even the quantitative extent of its resources.

Its second relation to economics is in terms of the stuff out of which today's productions are made. The whole post-revolutionary development in Russia is itself dramatic. The spectacular change in the character of peasant life, with its great shifts of population, its tragedies and its achievements; the remarkable expansion of industry and its attendant crowding of cities, the upsurge of new social forces, sudden turns in social ideas; the confusing mixture of misery and enthusiasm, of individual cruelties and social idealism; the truly theatrical attempt to conquer the North with the elemental forces of nature in the rôle of villain and the whole Arctic as the backdrop:—these are the materials of Russian drama. And again they lead directly into the problems of the Russian economy. The job of the theatre is to clarify its objectives, to interpret its ideology, and to appraise its effect on life itself.

But these facts should not mislead the reader into thinking that *this study* is an attempt to approve the Russian régime or its organization or any of its objectives. It is rather an analysis (given the totalitarian conditions) of the effect of a régime of the Russian type on the drama in terms of an analysis of the forces which impinge upon the drama, and an appraisal of the results. It *must* not, therefore, be considered as ammunition for either the Russian propagandist or the Communist baiter.

The author has given his life to the study of the drama; he has had opportunity for direct observation and experience in the American, the French, and the Russian theatre; he has no axe to grind and is then in a position to make an objective study. This study will be of interest to all students of present dramatic trends and to those like myself who, having no competence whatever in the theatre field, are interested in the *Theatre at the Left* as an objective study of the effect of Russian economy upon one segment of Russian life.

JAMES H. SHOEMAKER

Department of Economics,
Brown University.

TO THOMAS CROSBY, JR.

A NEW THEATRE EMERGES

I

A New Theatre Emerges

THE OLD ADAGE about the east and the west and never the twain meeting is given the lie in the shadow of the ginger-bread Kremlin walls. All is a little confusing to the new comer. The Orient and the Occident not only meet, but they mingle and blend. Tibet and Western Europe walk down the streets of the Soviet capital arm in arm and pass the minarets of St. Basil, the modernistic red marble tomb of Lenin, and the skyscraper shafts of the New Moscow Hotel without one disturbing thought for the incongruity. The bells of the citadel ring out the quarter hours above the honk of auto horns and the babel of foreign tongues. East meets west; the middle ages rub shoulders with the twentieth century. Here is a new world of philosophy and action.

Even the theatres are different. Old methods of stagecraft survive alongside the most advanced mechanisms of the modern theatre world. The incomprehensible inwardnesses of experimental cults are tempered in the next block by the somewhat over-realistic practices of a determined naturalistic school. Okhlopkov invents a playhouse without a stage; Meyerhold conceives a play without scenery; the Vakhtangov looks for a sophistication in styles; the Gorki Art serenely follows the clear star of intimate reality. Tairov struggles to find a social relationship in Eugene O'Neill. But behind this confusion of forms and methods there is a design and a thoughtful plan. The Soviet theatre is original and different, not because it is bizarre and at times grotesque in expression, but because it is a theatre with a definite objective and a clearly defined purpose. That purpose is to build a Proletarian Culture.

To reduce all to the lowest common denominator? America knows something of that catastrophe. Too easily music can become jazz and swing; poetry can become the drivel of a columnist; dancing can become the black bottom; and pictorial art, the funnies. Proletarian Culture does not mean leveling. Indeed, the contrary hits nearer the center of truth. To raise the mass mind to an understanding of the best and to make true art a classless expression is the difficult and, as yet, unrealized ideal of the Soviet Theatre.

A classless culture is a culture of joint ownership. When a private theatre fails to do its work well, the audiences withdraw their patronage, and the enterprise comes to an end. There is no thought on the part of such audiences to do more than express disapproval; there is less thought of cooperating with the theatrical venture to improve its bills and the quality of its work. There is certainly no feeling that the company's failure is really the community's loss. It is very difficult to find any reason why the American audience should assume a responsibility for the success or failure of the commercial theatre. It is admittedly a business enterprise without civic importance. An adequate retort to the question "Why did you let the company fail?" would be "It is not my affair; it is not my company." But such an answer is not adequate when the theatre is class-less. The Soviet audience says, "It is OUR theatre." In that small word lies a world of difference.

It is *our* theatre. It does not depend upon a diamond circle or the Calvinistically predestined intelligentsia for patronage. It is not a theatre in which the balance in black outweighs the artistry, and in which civic value is lightly passed over or forgotten altogether. It is a theatre whose triumphs are the pride and whose defeats are the joint responsibilities of its audiences, for they are its owners. Its playwrights, its designers, its directors, its actors are common property. The artists belong to the people. Theatre is classless. It is the privilege of every citizen to help make it the best theatre in the world.

Now one might say, "This all sounds very chaotic to me. Aren't there a good many fingers in the pie?" There would be many too many fingers in the pie if there were not a pattern and a clearly defined series of objectives, which are the foundation stones of this Proletarian Culture. Lenin said: "Only with an exact knowledge of the culture created by mankind through his entire development, only upon the basis of reworking this knowledge, can we build a Proletarian Culture." Here is the key, knowledge. The theatre is a leaven for education. One can learn through the theatre. After an untutored old fellow in Moscow had seen his first play, he was asked how he liked it. "Good," he replied. "The theatre is good. You find out things there. You learn to understand things." The theatre of the Soviet Union is a theatre in which one learns.

And there are many things to learn in this new State. The ages of suffering which preceded the new régime are the illuminating heritage of the Soviet Union from the pages of history. The literature of the theatre itself has a vital contribution to make. There were mighty playwrights in the old days, Gogol and Fonvizin, Pushkin and Ostrovski, who record the

Russia that was and foreshadow the State that is to be. And in addition to the nationalistic figures are the world dramatists, who are the common artistic possession of nations, Shakspere, Schiller, Goldoni, and Molière. Proletarian Culture reworks the knowledge of the past, not with pedantic veneration for the old, but with the burning desire to drink deeply the full meaning of the glorious present. Antiques are valueless in the U. S. S. R. unless they contribute to workaday life.

Moving away from the ancient days, there is the more immediate past to be studied. The new theatre is anxious to explain the Revolution and to develop a fine feeling of loyalty for those who died that an old order might give place to a new. Through such plays as *The Armored Train, Storm, The Army Commander,* and *The Unknown Soldier,* the people experience afresh the October Days and the Civil War; the masses are brought closer to the heroes who suffered for the cause from the days of *Stenka Razin* to *The Last of the Turbins.*

Through the theatre the State campaigns for unification. The national minorities are a problem. Race prejudices and hatred can better be over- come if one part of the Union understands how the other part thinks. The folklore of the Caucasus becomes the weekday knowledge of the Leningrad worker; and the life of the Moscow streets is echoed in Tiflis and Baku.

There are perplexing questions of social and economic nature which the citizen must master. The women of the south have thrown aside their veils; the women of the industrial centers participate in the administration of a throbbing economy. A new woman comes into being. What does the State expect of her? Inga and Yarovaia personify the liberated woman for the people. The farm collective, the village collective, the difficulties of factory management—these and endless other problems are the engrossing concern of the Union. The theatre labors to foster a better understanding in the people, thereby consolidating the State and stimulating an increasing devotion to the Cause. The theatre is a living editorial of contemporary life in the Soviet Republic.

The old theatre knows this particular task only too well, for it is not the first time the theatre has been a classroom for the masses. After the drama was reborn, at the steps of the altar in the Dark Ages, it entered, through the miracle and mystery plays, the teaching service of the Mediæval Church. The theatre from the fall of the Roman Empire to the full bloom of the Renaissance was a theatre of didacticism. To recall the art of make-believe to the service of building a new philosophy and culture for the people is to tread a well-worn path. The wheel turns; the cycle is completed.

There is nothing new under the sun. To be a powerful force for the reëducation and reconstruction of men and women in a socialist state, to aid in the development of a Proletarian Culture is the primary objective of the Soviet Theatre.

Karl Marx taught that the philosophers had tried to interpret the world, that it was the work of the new socialism to change it. When this theory is applied to the fine arts, to many it appears that chaos is coming again. For centuries, æsthetics assumed that music, painting, the theatre were apolitical. The stage has been satisfied, together with the philosophers, to interpret the world, to reflect the world, but not to change the world. The application of the Marxian doctrine to the preserves of the drama necessitated a revolution in theatrical æsthetics. For the Soviet Union, the time had come when the bourgeois theatre had to go and a new standard of dramaturgy had to be discovered. The *Theatre at the Left* came into being.

There is a powerful school in Western Europe and especially in America which believes that the first function of drama is to entertain. This is the theory to which the "tired business man" subscribes. For him the theatre is release, and that is all he requires the theatre to provide. Now, surely, there is no reason why the theatre should not be entertaining, but it is an open question whether the theatre should not stimulate as well. To while away the time is one thing; to encourage mental growth and to increase æsthetic appreciation is another. The theatre which sets its goal at entertainment accomplishes little more than whiling away the time. The new theatre asks its audience to think and to reflect. It does not ask them to give up the cleansing force of laughter, nor does it deny them the catharsis of tears. The theatre of purpose does not, necessarily, taboo entertainment. It asks that entertainment shall be constructive and useful, not negative, certainly not passive. "To change the world, not to interpret it only!"

The new theatre does not believe in escapist art. Here, the drama is not an asylum for either playgoer or playwright who wishes to deny the world by hiding his head, ostrich like, that he may not see truth, and, therefore, since he cannot see, feel the strength to foreswear reality. "There is enough unpleasantness in life without seeing it in the theatre." To this thought there seems to be no answer if the speaker is *afraid of life*. But if one is to change the world, one cannot run away from the world. To refuse to look at the slums of our great cities does not rule them out of existence. To forget reality does not eliminate it. The new theatre believes that reality is more important than escape; that art which teaches

us to run away and forget lacks strength and virility, and encourages us
to fall into the ways of weakness and decadence.

Nor does the new theatre build its towers upon an art for art's sake
foundation, nor rear its red-flagged turrets into a thin rarified ether where
beauty is its own excuse for being. Art cannot exist apart from life, for it
pulses with life. Abstract beauty is not enough. To have form, line, color,
and design is not enough. Good art may have these qualities, but, in
addition, good art must have some utilitarian objective. Beauty is not its
own excuse for being, nor is the mystery of life, solved by a religious
hypothesis, an adequate explanation for existence. This is a theatre of
realism, a world stage reflecting the politics, the economics, the social
relationships of men. In the process of changing life, mere prettiness and
vague mysticism are not forces of strength but of weakness.

To change life, the theatre must stress the mass rather than the
individual. This does not mean that all plays must be plays of group action,
although such a method frequently inclines toward the ideal, which says
that the relationships of the individual bear little weight in society unless
they represent the very roots of the social structure. The old triangle play
is essentially a study of individuals, and, therefore, lacks social significance.
Elmer Rice's *Street Scene* represents the new method by which the triangle
may take on the color of true social importance. Kirschon in *Bread* demon-
strates how the triangle story may be subordinated to the mass ideology.
The new theatre does not deny individual emotions, nor does it feel that
they are unimportant. It does try to reëvaluate the old and to stimulate
mass responsibility.

The new theatre is opposed to imitation. In general, the moment an
art form becomes static, it starts to deteriorate rapidly. The new theatre
stresses the experimental and puts a premium on the creative. The slogan
well might be, "Always tomorrow." It is very easy in the theatre to bask
in the triumphs of yesterday. The American actor too often dwells on how
good he was in the last part. He is forever fingering his laurels. The ideal
of the new theatre is to let the dead past bury its dead. Work! Create!
Experiment! Leave the mistakes and the successes of yesterday. Find new
ways! Develop new methods! Make the theatre truly creative! Do not let
it become static, for then it will surely die. Leave imitation to the weak.
Art, to be strong and vital, must ever be progressive. The theatre is not
for weaklings.

Art that is strong and vital cannot be pessimistic. The new theatre
has no place in its busy ranks for the defeatist. Perhaps you remember the
old wheeze: "It is very cold in Russia. I am very unhappy. It is very cold

in Russia." Today, the reply would flare out: "Go out and cut wood; build a fire, and stop whimpering." The minor chords are no longer heard in the Soviet Theatre. Blatant trumpets now blast forth in major keys progress and faith in life. The new theory of the theatre has no place for the defeatist's philosophy. Chekhov gives way to Pogodin.

In less than two decades the Soviet Theatre emerges from the confusion of bloody Revolution, ghastly sabotage, and cruel civil war. It is not a theatre which desires to play its part merely as historian of the past, or photographer of current life. It is not a theatre for the escapist or the defeatist in art. It denies neither beauty, nor laughter, nor the free play of human emotions; but it does believe that these are factors in theatre, not ends in art. The new theatre is the possession of the people. The new theatre is experimental and creative. It is a theatre of revolution which is attempting to change the lives of men and not explain them. "ART is a weapon."

THE STATE AS PRODUCER

II

The State as Producer

THE THEATRE MANAGEMENT of the Platz Sverdlova is separated from that of Broadway by a gaping ravine of fundamental differences. The New York producers, without a unified policy either economic or artistic, raise and lower the curtain by a rule of thumb. The result is a cut and try series of plays which have only one common meeting point—the box office. The object of production, even though occasionally modified by a public-spirited Otto Kahn, is, frankly, to make money. The theatres of the Soviet Union, in contrast to this *laisser faire* business project, are operated through the government under a planned economy for the educational growth and development of a Proletarian State. The difference could not be more sharply defined, for the Union and America are poles apart in purpose. Art as a private financial enterprise stands rigidly opposed to art as a public cultural force.

The Baltic Republics, France, Poland, and Germany represent a middle ground. These nations have long been familiar with the principles of state subsidy, but none has ever placed all of its playhouses under one centralized control. The Soviet Union, therefore, has not invented a new system. Three centuries of nationalized theatre are symbolized in the red, gold, and crystal auditorium of the Comédie Française, which has echoed the despair of Polyeucte and the laughter of Scapin under Monarchy, Commune, and Republic. No—the Union is not original. Its program for state theatre is, in reality, only more comprehensive and elaborate than the respected and historic forerunners. Moscow has boldly expanded and adapted an accepted continental theory to meet the exacting requirements of a socialized society.

The Soviet Theatre exists as a subdivision of the Department of Education. Universities, research laboratories, conservatories, and technical and art museums are members of the same general family, which is fathered by that very important personage—the Commissar of Education. He is assisted in his Promethean task by a central committee, which in general aims to help all theatres to realize, without economic pressure, principles for which each stands. More specifically, the central committee promotes a policy which maintains a repertory of the classics (drama, opera, and ballet), sponsors experimentation in playwriting and production, trains actors in state schools, and encourages substantially non-professional groups in their dramatic activities. No interference with the artistic aims of production is tolerated, but a strict supervision of the repertory is maintained to protect the stage from heresies or contaminating counter-revolutionary doctrines.

The current productions of the program are not presented in "long run," a business reform established in the theatre world in the last century by Charles Kean, but function under the formerly popular repertory system so well known in the United States in pre-Civil War days, now outclassed in the race for a six months' Broadway "hit." The scheme of repertory is very simple. A large company is rehearsed and has on tap for performances five to fifty plays. Each night the curtain rises upon a different piece. There is no mad scramble by the management to rush the company through this store of dramatic fare which has been prepared. Popular demand and the readiness for competent performance determine the pace. Some plays reach the footlights only once or twice in a season; others are frequently acted. The turn of each year brings new pieces to the established program; old favorites are temporarily shelved; forgotten successes are restored to the boards in revivals; special performances mark memorable days. An incomplete list of plays on call at the Gorki Art Theatre may quicken the picture. Gorki: *Enemies, The Lower Depths, Bulychev;* Chekhov: *The Cherry Orchard, The Three Sisters;* Tolstoi: *Anna Karenina, Resurrection;* Ostrovski: *Storm, Talents and Admirers, A Warm Heart;* Gogol: *Dead Souls;* Afinogenev: *Fear;* Ivanov: *The Armored Car;* Kirschon: *Bread;* Beaumarchais: *The Marriage of Figaro;* Lope de Vega: *The Gardener's Dog.*

A specimen announcement for a week at the same theatre might read like this: Monday, *The Cherry Orchard;* Tuesday, *Anna Karenina;* Wednesday Matinée, *The Marriage of Figaro;* Wednesday Evening, *The Cherry Orchard;* Thursday, *Bread;* Friday, *Bread;* Saturday Afternoon, *The Armored Car;* Saturday Evening, *The Cherry Orchard.* The next week the selection of plays would possibly include pieces presented the week previous, or perhaps none of them. The demands of the audience and the expediences of production would determine the program.

Surely this old-time system of theatre management is not without certain advantages, the most important of which is to train a theatre-bent public to count a good play as a good friend and not regard an evening in the theatre as a passing experience. "I have seen that one," is a frequent

comment when the long run controls the dramatic output. The repertory
system encourages the audience to develop an appetite for plays through
familiarity with the theatre fare. Music lovers do not hear the *Fifth
Symphony* once and then banish it forever. Musical appreciation grows
through recurrence and repetition of the emotional experience. The plays
of Ostrovski and Shakspere do not lose their savor through pleasant
familiarity. The State Theatres in repertory provide an opportunity for
the Soviet audience to become really acquainted with the drama, old and
new. Knowledge and love of the stage are considered cultural power in
the U. S. S. R.

Moscow is a city of many theatres in which over fifty established
companies are playing through their repertories each season. Not infre-
quently does the playgoer find several groups billing the same play in
their current programs. Such an occurrence, far from being a misfortune,
provides a fine opportunity to study a play in two or three variant interpretations in one winter. America may recall the delightful experience of
seeing Gielgud and Howard battle for supremacy in the Denmark scene
at rival theatres, separated by a few city blocks. Certainly the mystery of
Shakspere did not lose its magic by watching each of these stirring Hamlets
in turn. Such an experience is common in the neighborhood of the Sverdlova, and Moscow is only one of several seething centers of theatrical
activity in the Soviet Union.

The production of plays in repertory requires hard work and plenty
of it. It is no easy matter to learn, rehearse, perform so many bills and to
have them come glibly to the tongue at call. It is no easy matter to strike
the settings and properties, pack away the costumes after the matinée of
The Cherry Orchard, and to reset with all hands on deck for the evening
performance of *The Armored Train* at a little past seven o'clock—for the
curtain rises early in Moscow. Such strenuous theatre requires precision,
efficiency, and discipline not only for the actors but for the entire staff.
To compass such a pretentious program each theatre becomes a veritable
commune within its own walls. The Gorki Art in Moscow maintains an
acting company considerably larger than that of the New York Metropolitan Opera, and, when technical crew is added to the artists, the number
of tovarish workers far exceeds the size of the student body of Amherst
College. There is, of course, great gain made in the name of solid artistic
performances when an entire group through years of intimate association
learns to work together. There is a greater gain made when such groups
are guided by high idealism and singleness of purpose.

Idealism, to produce results, must be coupled with skill. Actors, like musicians, should know the tools of their trade. To provide trained labor for the repertory theatre, specialized schools or technicums of the stage arts open their doors to student actors. Under the best of instructors they are taught the routines of the playhouse and drilled in a background of general education as well. They are trained in native language, literature, music, dancing, foreign tongues, and history. Such courses of study usually cover a four-year period. If the young student completes his course (it is very easy for him to fail), he is then ready to try his strength in one of the repertory companies, not as Constantine in *The Seagull,* but more likely in a three-line bit in *Tzar Feydor.* If he is a promising worker, the great rôles are not far ahead; if he is a loyal worker, he will never be without a job. Unlike the unfortunates who wear out shoe leather tramping up and down Broadway or about Piccadilly Circus searching for the engagement which is just around the corner, the Soviet actor finds himself ever socially secure. There is plenty of work. The constant increase in programs absorbs more artists than the schools can supply.

The Soviet actor is not a waste product in society, partly because he approaches his trade fortified with knowledge. Perhaps there would be fewer unemployed in the American theatre if many of those who call themselves artists were artists in more than name. The Soviet actor through formal training and continued study of his art naturally develops into a superior craftsman. But his job does not end there, for he is more than a technical expert; he is also a teacher and a social worker. To excel as an artist is his duty to the theatre; to contribute tirelessly to building a Proletarian Culture is his arduous responsibility to the State. This he assumes not as a burden but as a privilege.

Those who are masters are expected to instruct others. Olympus is not a luxurious asylum; it is a school. A classroom history of instruction in the Soviet Theatre discloses the unselfish record of tireless effort on the part of the greatest of the great—Stanislavsky, Tairov, Meyerhold. Nor does social responsibility end with teaching. There are non-professional dramatic clubs to be organized, directed; there are courses of lectures to be given; there is the cooperative work in the public schools; there are the smaller theatres in the provinces which must have expert advice and super-vision. All of these and many other duties are part of the Soviet actor's business. His life is a many-sided activity. He does not belong to a leisure class. He is a Comrade Worker, laboring to develop a Proletarian Culture in a Workers' State.

And his rewards? There are wages. There may be some special privileges which are added with advancing years. Kipling said "each for the joy of the working." The Soviet theatre folk do get a joy out of the job. As the years go by, now and again a worker is especially marked by the State. He may be made an "Honored Artist of the Republic" for faithful service; he may be made a "Master of the Art of the Republic," for long and signal service; for exceptional and distinguished service, he may become an "Honored Artist of the People." A few, very few, have been so honored; Stanislavsky is one. Is it not reminiscent of the Athenian lad who ran the course for a laurel branch?

The government as producer encourages its workers to experiment— a policy which is not common in the American commercial theatre. Possibly box office managements are reasonably and justly afraid. On this side of the Atlantic too often the unusual appears radical or extravagant, and the new is labeled meaningless or absurd. A revolt from old and conventional artistic forms too frequently is regarded as blasphemy or an unbridled attempt to unstring Orpheus's lyre. Styles in art, however, may change as well as those in clothes. It is possible for Dickens's spirit of reform to become antiquated nineteenth century sociology. The existence of a Keats did not preclude the possibility of a Vachel Lindsay. It is doubtful if any temple remains a joy forever. If art reflects the temper and spirit of its day, the progressive expressions of contemporary life deserve at least hearing and tolerant consideration, even though they fail eventually to gain the permanency of already accepted modes. Amy Lowell and Cézanne were needed to liberalize poetry and painting, even though Boston found each "too absurd" for a period. The Soviet theatre believes that static art is bad. Experimentation keeps the eternal flame burning.

To build a classless society, the Soviet theatre accepts the belief that the race is in the running and the goal is ever ahead. All successes of the moment become relative in value, for the determination to extend the borders of theatre arts is the hoped-for end. "There must be a better way" —the stage murmurs to itself. The feverish press to penetrate unexplored possibilities of the craft continues. With open mind and unhampered by ghastly terror of financial failure, experimentation is made easy. Rival schools of theory carry on their work in peace. Whatever may be their differences of approach, the audience, confident that progress in the theatre is their honest aim, watches willingly and discusses freely the merits of these rival schools.

There are two master courses of dramaturgy in the Soviet theatre. They have been termed the left and the right, the conservative and the radical, the naturalistic and the impressionistic. Could they not be called, without too much confusion, the outward and the inward schools? Each has its high priests, prophets, traitors, and sworn enemies. Sometimes it is difficult to tell just what a particular producer or actor is attempting, but, after a little, it becomes evident that one of the two great dramatic philosophies has him in thrall, though he may himself be unaware he is under its spell. Both of these cults seek truth. Each is confident that it has found the most expressive and effective way.

Outwardness can easily be associated with the photographic point of view and with naturalism—although the devotees of the faith persist in violent denial of such an assertion. The observer looks at the world about him and realizes that there swims before his eyes a complex scheme. He tries to record in art forms what he sees. He is impressed by the numberless details which he struggles to reproduce with infinite, painstaking care. The significant purposes of each minute part in this baffling picture puzzle, and the relationships of each tiny piece to the other cry out for analysis. And then, without permitting the necessary technical mechanisms to be seen, a process of orderly assembling of the parts begins, and, at great length, art, guided by understanding, has reconstructed life. Nature is truth. The theatre of illusion emerges.

The inwardist is also seeking truth. He sees a tree in this confused world, but lets his mind wander to springtime sap and summer rain. He does not study the details of a leaf, but his mind's eye pierces the mysteries of the soil, and then, vital roots, stretching out beneath the too obvious grass, are no longer hidden to him. His vision tries to conquer invisibility. The exact relationship of the parts is extremely important to this inwardist too, but he denies that these complex crossings and counter-crossings can be caught by simple photographic reproduction. He is often forced to create new planes of action and spheres of visualization to project his inclusive thought. At this point he discovers that the mechanisms of art are his greatest helpers. He is proud of his aids and does not try to hide them. He does not care how distorted and jagged the pieces of the outward picture become if the inward truth is, as he feels it, more clearly expressed. Inwardness is truth; art must attempt to express the intangible realities as well as the naturalistic certitudes of life. The theatre of disillusionment emerges.

At the fore of the theatre illusionists stands the Gorki Art of Moscow, led by the world-renowned figures, Stanislavsky and Danchenko. Since 1898 this theatre has been the final authority for the realists during Imperialistic and Soviet régimes alike. Here is the eternal Mecca for those who seek a life on the stage more real than life itself. This group under high and inspired leadership has cut the cloth to suit the vicissitudes of Imperial Court, Revolution, Civil War, and Collective Government. The theatre has never, however, wavered in its artistic standards or in its exalted purpose.

In a half century Stanislavsky here has evolved a theory of acting which, if judged from naturalistic standards and proficiency in analysis of minute relationships, is beyond criticism. Here the *mise en scène,* the *ensemble,* the *dècor* always are the last word in psychological harmoniza-tion. The Gorki Art Theatre well may boast that it has succeeded in making the theatre untheatrical by removing the fourth wall and turning actors into living men and women. Through its tried years of service it has encouraged and presented the best of realistic playwrights. Chekhov first became popular within these walls; Gorki's *Lower Depths* is associated, almost inseparably, with this theatre. Once the Revolution had spent its fury, Ivanov's super-naturalistic *Armored Train* found understanding interpreters here.

The influence of this theatre and its leaders cannot be satisfactorily measured. Most of the distinguished Russian actors and producers have at one time or another come under its spell. Vakhtangov, Popov, and Meyerhold—exponents of rival schools—had their training here. Though they have wandered far from the theatre of illusion, the spirit of the Gorki Art breaks through in their most heretical endeavors. Thousands of miles from the Kremlin towers, Broadway unwittingly falls frequently under the mighty shadow of the grand old men of Moscow. Through them the psychological synthesis of acting and setting has been achieved.

At æsthetic sword points with the theories of illusion and intimate acting is the theatre of Vsevolod Meyerhold. This mad genius of the stage is difficult to follow, for he is ever changing his approach to production that he may come closer, as he sees it, to the inward truth. He has been influenced by the Orient, by the theatre of ancient Greece; he has found Shakspere and the stage of the Elizabethans stimulating; and the court theatre of the Grand Monarch has intrigued him. He is opposed to natural-ism, he shies at symbolism, and he hopes vaguely to create a worthy medium through which he can reveal to his cherished audience the ultimate truth and relationships of life which outward shows of stagecraft distort and disguise. His primary and thoroughly honest ambition is to rouse his audiences with deep, elemental, emotional reactions, which he believes lie hidden in the play script. To do this he ignores psychological character-ization and creates types; he discards established routines of stagecraft and projects his plays beyond the restricting arch of the proscenium into the laps of the audience. He feels that he is completely justified in tampering unmercifully with the text of the play if, thereby, he can intensify the emotional meaning of the author. If the whim strikes him, he tears down the act drop, and in a flash restores the curtain again without explanation.

When the Revolution came, he found himself, because of his uncon-ventional methods, the chief of those bent on the annihilation of the old bourgeois theatre. In those uncertain years, he passed through the phases of futurism, constructivism, cubism, and all the other "isms." He found the psychological system of acting too exacting for his interpretations and he created bio-mechanics and the constructivist actor which for a time seemed to give a greater flexibility to performers and stage business. He used music—not incidental or cue music—as part of all his productions, sometimes creating a pseudo-operatic score for the play. He frequently refused to submit to historical exactitude in costuming, because he felt that too much attention to the realistic externals clouded the clearness of the meaning from the spectators. As time passed, he became less and less blatant in his program of annihilation of the middle-class stage. Today he has given up his excesses, but he has not lost his spirit or unconventionality. He wills to create a new dramatic truth of high emotional content. Markov believes that Meyerhold most nearly approached his ideal in the production of *The Magnificent Cuckold*. This was early in his revolutionary career. Can the storm have spent its fury?

Meyerhold also approaches the theatre through mass drama. His interest is persistently focused upon the audience and its reactions to the play. He does not like to have the actors separated from the spectators by either an imaginary or an actual curtain line. He believes the emotional force of the scene should penetrate to the auditorium and be experienced by audience as well as by actors. "The spectators should not observe, they should share in the play"—is his theory. In this respect he becomes a priest of the drama of participation, a return to the theatre of Athens and to the Miracle and Mystery plays of the Middle Ages.

His distinguished pupil Okhlopkov, formerly director of the Krassnaya-Pressnya Theatre in Moscow, has succeeded in carrying this note of mass participation to some triumphant conclusions. Gorki's *Mother* has been most effectively produced by him with no stage at all. The action takes place on a platform in the central area of the auditorium. In a like fashion he presents Stavsky's *At a Run*. For *Othello* he builds a ribbon-like runway around the audience, and on this doughnut-like structure the business of Venice and Cyprus unfolds.

The use of such methods to emphasize participation may reasonably appear bizarre and extravagant. Okhlopkov is not attempting, however, to be different or arty. Both pupil and master of the counter-realistic school are overly sincere in their struggle to break with the conventional theatre. It is not difficult to quibble with interpretation as far as that goes. One may quibble with the interpretations of realism. It is very difficult on the other hand to deny the effectiveness of these unusual methods. Seeing is believing. Conversion is inevitable when Meyerhold or Okhlopkov open wide the floodgates of emotion and the inward message swirls out and overwhelms the spectator.

Another inwardist or counter-realist leader is Alexander Tairov of the Kamerny Art Theatre, who shares with Meyerhold the battle-shock against the stage of illusion, but who, beyond that point, makes his advances with original theories of theatre-craft. Tairov contends that the producer may catch elusive truth through symbol and abstraction. He believes that the mechanical qualities of the theatre in themselves have a high æsthetic value; that music, movement, voice, design, picturization are in themselves elements of legitimate stage value. His theatre first of all should *be theatre*. The world of make-believe is wholly sufficient within itself. In a former time he vaguely prattled an æsthetic jargon which was dimly reminiscent of the school of Gordon Craig. In the present time it is rumored that he is seeking, not, as formerly, for the dramatization of divorced beauty, which now might be considered counter-revolutionary, but for the isolation and abstraction of human emotions and their social relationships.

Could it be that Tairov is really an æsthete of the first water, madly struggling, in his search for a happy compromise between his old-admitted worship of remote, symbolic beauty and the harsher code devised by Soviet dramaturgy? Whatever personal adjustment the dictatorship of the Proletariat may have forced upon him, *The Optimistic Tragedy* and *The Egyptian Nights* are proof enough that his new æstheticism teems with theatrical virility. Tairov stands as a sane force against naturalism whether he is probing the native social relationships in a vital interpretation of Vishnevsky or revealing an unusual but plausible meaning in *The Hairy Ape* or *Desire Under the Elms*.

As Tairov has found a foreign playwright like O'Neill an invaluable medium through which to clarify his theories, so too the flourishing school founded by Eugene Vakhtangov and carried on by his devoted disciples after his untimely death in 1922 has found especial favor in production through the imported scripts of Schiller, Shakspere, and Gozzi. Though the Vakhtangov is generally catalogued "a theatre of compromise," its leanings to the left are so obvious that it may safely be listed with the counter-illusionary group. Each play must be interpreted in the method best suited to its content, says the school, for all is neither inwardness nor outwardness. All approaches must be utilized to arrive at truth. Sir Roger de Coverley admitted there was much to be said on both sides of the question.

To some this Horatian credo may seem an adequate charting of course. To others the Vakhtangov may seem to sail close to the borders of sardonic cartooning. Its guiding artistic principle appears to be exaggeration of the emotions, the make-up, the speech, the gestures, the setting, and through these distorted or over-accentuated elements to present to the audience a series of vivid contrasts and at times strikingly ironic pictures of life. Do not be misled. There is no element of burlesque here; there *is* an element of the bizarre. The effect of a Vakhtangov production may be compared with that produced when the artist squints his eye to see more clearly the absolute color values in the landscape. To utilize such a squinting method in dramatic interpretation results in most startling effects. Just as the cartoon aids us to catch at a glance the idiosyncrasies of character, so the Vakhtangov theory of the theatre enables us to appreciate the sharp, hard values of life. There is little milk of human kindness in this system, but eccentric though it may be, it constitutes a masterly relief from the over-emphasis of meticulous naturalism.

The Gorki Art, the Kamerny, the Meyerhold, the Krassnaya-Pressnya, the Vakhtangov represent the powerful master plants through which the two main philosophies of Soviet theatre are expressing themselves in the Kremlin city. There are many other theatres in Moscow. The First and Second Studios, the Maly (the Comédie Française of the old régime), and the musical laboratories of Stanislavsky and Danchenko follow the traditions established by the real parent of psychological synthesis—the Moscow Art. The Workers' Theatres, the Theatre of the Red Army, and the Theatre of Revolution incline to the teachings of Meyerhold. Each group, however, maintains its own individuality and works out the problems of production in its own way. It must not be forgotten, moreover, that although Moscow is the great theatrical capital, the experimentation goes forward in Leningrad, Karkov, and Tiflis, and that the smallest cities are also making their contribution to the whole, though their inspiration may be traced back to the Sverdlova.

One of the greatest strengths of the *Theatre at the Left* is that it is not all cut to a pattern. The desire for progress makes it impossible for this creative stage to be satisfied with any static æsthetics. Modifications of the two main currents come with the changing of the moon. It would be difficult to speak with finality, but a grain of truth there may be in the passing thought that the outwardists influence the tradition of acting to a greater degree than the inwardists; that the theatre of disillusionment, in turn, guides, through subtle inroads against conventional stagecraft, the course of production methods. Whatever the final judgment might be on this point, it is evident that the last two decades have not passed without witnessing practically every conceivable stage theory actively represented in the State Theatres of the Soviet Union.

The Soviet audience is proud of its theatre. Scattering attendance is unknown; vacant seats are rare. The public demand for more plays is ever increasing. To attend a performance in Leningrad, Moscow, or Tiflis is to witness an intent, enthusiastic body of spectators which constitutes a cross-section of Soviet life. The excitement is akin to that collegiate spirit traditional at an American football game. The motley mass in the Soviet playhouse, like the motley mass in the American stadium, has learned to participate.

This Soviet audience wills to watch, but it does not always lend its approval. Critical to a fault, it is too willing, if anything, to discuss and argue the excellencies or the shortcomings of actor, producer, and playwright. The foyers buzz with argument during each entr'act. It is not always a well-mannered audience. It hisses, and murmurs, and sometimes talks out of turn, but it is ever alert and attentive to the content of the play. A progressive theatre in which well-trained actors stir the emotions *should* fill its seats. "It is our theatre and we will make it the best theatre in the world." Where there is a will, there is a way. The Proletarian State enters the scene as its own Producer.

EDUCATING AN AUDIENCE

III

Educating an Audience

ARLY EACH SEPTEMBER, from dawn until long after dark, an eager, happy, seemingly endless procession marches in well-ordered ranks through the Red Square of the Soviet capital. Platoon after platoon pauses for a few seconds before the Lenin Tomb to be reviewed by the People's Commissars and then passes on to make room for the thousands of waiting marchers. Bands are playing, groups are singing, banners are flying. Traffic waits good naturedly, and cheers from the crowded street fill the air. Hour after hour the procession files on and on. These are not soldiers, nor are they factory workers. They are children. This is International Youth Day. To see the gay demonstration is to believe readily that the Soviet is interested in its boys and girls; to watch these thousands of happy but determined young faces is to believe that the youth of the Union is interested in its State. This colorful, merry pageant symbolizes the slogan of the U. S. S. R., "education through art," especially education through the art of the theatre—for International Youth Day in Moscow is in itself theatre.

Theatres for the children were not unheard of in Russia before the World War. Desultory and sporadic performances for young spectators have been sparingly indulged in for the last fifty years, but the first organized effort to make the theatre a part of child education and to have that effort sponsored by the State as a coordinate unit with the public schools, is one of the most progressive and constructive contributions of the Soviet Union to modern youth training. In 1919 Pascar, an Austrian lady, made some headway with a children's theatre in Moscow, but the real work of planning and organizing and establishing such a theatre permanently was the heroic task of a young girl, who in Revolutionary Days was a mere child herself, but who today has won the recognition of the Soviet Union as an "Honored Artist of the Republic."

Natalia Satz has seen her dream of a professional theatre for children materialize from an unnoticed, struggling, but enthusiastic group in one large metropolitan center to a state enterprise which now maintains over one hundred theatres throughout vast territories of the Union. In the capital alone there are today the Central Children's Theatre, The Khalatov

Theatre of Children's Books, The Theatre of Young Spectators, The Workers' Children's Theatre, and the Central State Theatre of Young Spectators. The purpose of these theatres is to aid the public schools with their routine educational work, to develop appreciation of the fine arts, and to stimulate creative instinct. These theatres are real theatres. In no sense are they makeshift attempts at play production. They are not the kindly, well-meaning contribution of amateurs to the leisure-time activities. The best is none too good for the children. Good art again becomes a very subtle weapon in building a Proletarian Culture.

Long since parents and educators have recognized the need for children's books. Some attention has been given to children's music and art. In America little time has been wasted on the children's theatre, Clara Major's courageous attempts notwithstanding. Adults have been content to believe either that there is no need for the children to learn through the theatre, that the cinema is adequate, or that an occasional performance of Shakspere is stimulating enough. Now, with proper reverence due to genius, Shakspere is certainly not distinguished as a children's dramatist. Even *Midsummer Night's Dream,* the standby for juveniles, is not all fireflies and a bank where the wild thyme grows. The good is not always best if it comes too early. The first problem confronting the Soviet Children's Theatre is to discover the type of theatrical performance which most satisfactorily stimulates in youth a sympathetic inclination toward the fine arts.

What does the child mind crave? The answer to this question is the commencement of the project. The directors of the Children's Theatres are sensible enough not to predetermine what the child mind *ought* to crave. There is a nice distinction here, often overlooked by educators. All children do not ask the same questions or have the same interests. The directors find that age differences, sex differences, and nervous or temperamental differences complicate considerably the problem of creating a repertory. To cope with this difficulty, the theatre supervisors analyze the interests of the children from these three points of approach: age, sex, temperament. Puck and Bottom do not fit the bill just because they are classic characters. The child in the Soviet Union has to wait until he is ready to be exposed to Shakspere before he sits through his first performance of *The Midsummer Night's Dream.* "Everything in due time," says the theatre of Natalia Satz.

To analyze the interests of young spectators requires the friendly, intimate cooperation of theatre, children, teachers, and parents. The youngsters are encouraged to write letters to their playhouse telling in their own way how the ballet, the drama, or the operetta which they recently saw impressed them. Parents are urged to inform the theatre directors regularly concerning the reactions of the boys and girls in the home to the plays seen. The children are watched closely during the performances, and signs of over-stimulation, lack of interest, and normal enthusiasms are recorded. And so home, school, and theatre are sympathetically united in a sane, thoughtful effort to ferret out what the child mind craves, understands, and appreciates in dramatic fare and what it should be fed. This popular artistic cooperation of parents, actors, teachers, and children makes possible the Union's novel adventure in education through drama. Again—it is "our" theatre.

The stacks of material collected through this close cooperation might remain so much documentary evidence to collect dust in the files were there not those who synthesize and interpret all the data gathered. At this point a body of experts becomes necessary. A staff of trained child psychologists advises the directors and managers and assists in selecting or creating the repertory. These skilled workers are not "called in" for a professional consultation. There is no time for them to be engaged on the side in another job. The work in the theatre is not a fad or a pastime for them when the daily routine is over. The psychological division is an integral and indispensable part of the organization of the children's theatres without which the success of the project would be doomed at the start.

The criterion of a successful play, as determined by these experts, is not necessarily the amount of applause which it is given by its youthful audience. The spontaneous reaction of approval is only a partial test of true value. Does the spirit of the drama find itself reflected in the daily lives of the young spectators? Sometimes weeks pass before a definite estimate of the worth of the performance can be adequately and finally recorded. Do not forget that these plays are *not* produced primarily to entertain or divert the children during a rainy Saturday afternoon when parents or teachers or nurses are worn ragged and want an hour's rest. Success is measured by the stimulative effect of the representation. The Marxian philosophy is again in evidence—not to understand but to change human beings. The Children's Theatre in the Soviet Union attempts to understand its youthful audience only that it may be more efficient in developing character. Art can be a very subtle weapon.

Participation in the performance is not less important in the children's than in the adult's theatre. Training the boys and girls to merge themselves in the activities of "their" playhouse increases the sense of mass ownership and helps to emphasize the "carry over" until the next performance.

Children are taught to organize their own theatre parties. They are not forced to attend by well-meaning parents and teachers. The children send delegates to the theatre councils. Naturally, the advice and suggestions which they offer their elders are not always followed to the letter, but the young folk learn to feel a responsibility for their theatre and are provided with a forum in which to raise their voices, which often suggest plans of such merit that they are incorporated in the policy. Through such a plan the children get their first lessons in social relationships, civic management, and art appreciation. All this may appear a sugar-coated pill to the severe critic, but the results amply justify this time-consuming method in the eyes of the Central Committee of Education.

A more active means of participating in the spirit of the play is frequently provided by the performance itself. There are guessing plays, word plays, and voting plays for the younger children. The guessing plays and the word plays are a sort of animated anagram or elaborated charade. It is not difficult to imagine how expert and flexible the actors must be in pantomimic technique and the spontaneous routines of the old *commedia dell'arte* to meet the exacting requirements of this extemporaneous and impromptu theatre. In the voting plays, a problem is set for children in the opening scenes; then, the audience is asked to decide the course of the drama. The actors adapt the dialogue and plot to meet the conclusion selected by the vote of their youthful spectators. Participation trains the children not only to observe, but to think as well about the play which they are attending.

One of the most exciting pieces of this type is *The Rapscallion* by Bochina. Linka Smekhov is a happy young pioneer, but he has a mind of his own. A young woman, Tipa Motilina, is the adult leader of his group. She does not understand that children have original and often highly-colored ideas, nor does she sense that frequently it is better to direct and encourage misguided initiative than to condemn it as insubordination. She spends the class periods in discussion and talk, but fails to keep the active children occupied. Linka falls into difficulty with Tipa. She misinterprets his pranks and grows in the belief that the boy lacks cooperation. The situation becomes more and more strained until the unhappy youngster is brought to account for his bad spirit and faces expulsion from his Pioneer group. A juvenile trial scene follows. "What shall we do with Linka?" someone on the stage asks. The young Pioneers in the audience supply the answer. With the same alacrity with which American and English boys and girls used to reply in the old days to the plea of Peter Pan for Tinker

Bell's life, the Soviet youth never fail to exonerate Linka. Of course this particular play does not strain the ingenuity of the actors.

To develop the spirit of individual creation is more difficult than to stimulate mass participation. This often *does* tax the ingenuity of the directors. One excellent solution is the theatre art galleries, where costume plates, scene designs, and pictures illustrating the repertory, all drawn by the children, are displayed. Only the best go onto the walls for exhibition. Each child is encouraged to try to express himself, but the spirit of competition and "achievement through excellence" which later makes Stakhanovite workers is stressed for the seven- and eight-year-olds.

Besides pictorial art work there are dances, songs, and games derived from the material of the plays. The foyer of the theatre is a merry playground before the curtain rises and during the intermissions at the Children's Theatres. The directors try to coordinate these song and dance interludes with the dramatic theme of the day. For instance, if the play were about the life of the French Court at the time of Molière, the young spectators would be taught dance steps and musical rounds, relating the spirit of long ago with that of contemporary life. Through participation in singing, dancing, and painting, the children's minds are attuned to the temper and meaning of the play which a few minutes later will thrill them on the stage. The scheme is almost flawless on paper. Of course, it does not always work one hundred per cent efficiently. That would be claiming too much for any plan.

At this moment someone is likely to raise the question: "When and where does all this activity go on?" The theatres for young spectators are not one-day-a-week enterprises. The curtain rises and falls in the children's playhouses with the same regularity with which it rises and falls in the theatres for adults. There are daily performances, and sometimes two. In addition to the program at the regular playhouses, special performances are given at schools, factories, and farm collectives. Especial effort is made to bring plays to the rural districts where the conditions will not as yet permit the founding of a permanent company. During the summer months, groups from the central theatre are sent out on tour, that the work of the winter may be continued in the children's camps and vacation centers.

There are also performances for the hospitals. Special plays must be devised for this purpose which require little scenery and easily accommodate themselves to the peculiar needs of those invalided youngsters who can never come to the central playhouses. Special plays are also written for the blind, and at regular intervals these children, who must learn to see with ears, are brought to the theatre, for it is their theatre too. A physical handicap must not keep the unfortunates from thinking of the stage as "ours."

The buildings where plays are presented are carefully designed and decorated to appeal to the imagination of their youthful owners and to make them feel at home. Worn out and dilapidated adult playhouses are not converted to stop-gap the children's needs, nor are all these theatres constructed according to one cut-and-dried civic blueprint. The architects for the Young People's Theatre in Leningrad stressed in their plans a play-house which would encourage participation. Seats rise about a platform extending farther than usual into the auditorium. The result reminds one of the demonstration laboratories in a medical school. Naturally, the back-stage is very shallow; the forestage is overlarge. The purpose in the designer's mind is to bring actors into intimate association with the audience. Unlike this amphitheatre, the Moscow children's stages are most conventional in appearance. Though different in physical plan, each of the theatres discourages any attempt to fool the children. This is not real life; it is theatre. The drama should stimulate the *imagination* but should not be confused with reality. It should help to *explain* reality, however.

Natalia Satz says: "Every performance of a theatre for children must bring something new, or else succeed in throwing new light on the usual, the everyday—making it deeper, more significant. Every successive per-formance for children must transfer each spectator from the level on which he stood before seeing the play to the next level higher." This is rugged idealism. To manipulate such a theory into the concrete, the playwrights must be willing and ready.

What are these special plays which craftsmen like Agnev, Rosanov, Satz, and Shestakov write to meet these demands? What are these plays for which musicians like Polovinkin compose scores which sometimes are heard beyond the orchestra pit of the Children's Theatres on the concert stage? Are they different from other theatre pieces? First of all, these plays must never talk down to the children. They must be interesting and thrill-ing if possible. The plays generally meet these "musts" most adequately. He would, indeed, be a supersophisticated adult who failed to get a kick out of these performances of children's drama. To be sure, all the plays have a central didactic purpose or idea—"Tendenz" drama if you wish. They are concerned with the problems of social justice, heroic idealism, and sacrifice for the mass; they aim to direct the youthful imagination through allegory; they try to inform without being pedantic; they attempt to make the Soviet ethics understandable and human without unnecessary preaching.

Zayitzki's *Robin Hood* appeals to the fancy of the Soviet boy as well as to that of American or English lads. The central theme emphasizes social justice rather than adventure. The well-remembered figures of the Greenwood become heroes of the people, fighting against economic injustice in a society where the Sheriff of Nottingham epitomizes the tyrannical brutality of the selfish individualism over the masses. The old ballads stressed this idea too. The Soviet interpretation is, to a degree, historical and reactionary rather than radical. Do not think, however, that the romance, which children love the world over, has been entirely deleted. The men of Lincoln are as merry in Great Russia as ever they were in Sherwood. The adventure still has all of the snap and bite which have held youth from play these generations past. Robin Hood in the Soviet Theatre becomes more purpose or class conscious than on its native soil, and that is about all.

Social justice is also the theme of *The Negro Boy and the Monkey*, the just fame of which has spread beyond the borders of the Union. This is a pantomime play, with music, for the younger children, which starts off with a prologue in which the pleasant Negro Girl says: "Here there will be no talking. Why should there be? You couldn't understand negro language anyway. But the pleasant Negro Girl will explain everything to you. She speaks Russian and reads Russian too. So after the show you should write a letter to the pleasant Negro Girl and tell her how you liked *The Negro Boy and the Monkey*." Then the play begins.

Nagua, a little black boy, has a pet monkey to whom he owes his life. But Yirka, the monkey, is stolen out of the jungle by a bad circus manager and carried far away to Moscow. Little Nagua starts on a perilous journey to find his pet. It is a long way to Moscow, and many adventures beset him along the route. Of course, he finds his animal friend before the final curtain is rung down. This topsy-turvy retelling of Androcles and the lion points out to boys and girls the foolishness of race prejudices and the social injustice which easily arise through misunderstanding our fellow human beings. Natalia Satz is responsible for the libretto of this popular play. The score was composed by the distinguished Polovinkin, who has contributed so much music to the Children's Theatres.

In contrast to the whimsical fancy of *The Negro Boy and the Monkey* is the heroic realistic story of youth, *Timoska's Mine,* a tale about a young Pioneer who saved from ruin a valuable mine which the saboteurs had planned to blow up. Every child who sees a performance of this melodramatic play wants to be like Timoska and serve the State as loyally as he did. More imaginative and idealized but like in purpose is *Hiawatha,* who wears his feathers in the Soviet Union as an inspired boy chief, sacrificing all that his people may be happy. This type of play stresses the subordination of the individual for the good of the mass, a lesson which *every boy and girl* in the Union must learn at an early age if he hopes to be a happy citizen in a Proletarian State.

Children's plays frequently deal with the fairy story. The Marxian specialists do not believe that such dramas should fill too large a space in the utilitarian repertory, but reluctantly admit that *Puss in Boots* might be useful in training and stimulating the imagination. The youngest spectators must be taught rigorously, here as elsewhere, to distinguish fable from reality. For all that, Soviet children like plays of unreality. They seem to crave them. Children all over the world do. Two plays, very different in theme, will illustrate this type of youthful spectator's drama—*The Tales from Anderson* and *Chronomobile*.

The first retells the familiar old story of the foolish king who is dressed in nakedness by his clever, mischievous tailors. They convince the stupid ruler that the wise will see him clothed in magnificence, but the dull will not be able to see his fine garments at all. The king looks at himself in a mirror. He is mildly surprised to view his nakedness, but, naturally, will not admit the fatal fact, even to himself. All his courtiers are too well trained in lordly deceit to tell the king the truth. Finally a little boy proclaims with relish that the proud monarch is as naked as the day he was born. In confusion and shame, the king, having lost the respect of his subjects, runs away from his kingdom.

In *Chronomobile,* a gifted professor invents a miraculous device by which human beings may move forward and back in time and space—very much as they do in Maxwell Anderson's *Star Wagon,* or in *Berkeley Square.* In *Chronomobile* the youth of the Revolutionary and Civil War days take a trip to the future and see, as the playwright tells it, the glorious times that are to be when a socialist state is no longer a dream but an established reality for the Union and for the world. Through diminutive dramas such as these, the Soviet child is trained to let his imagination wander in a world of make-believe where the building of a powerful state for the people is the principal castle in Spain. The purpose is never forgotten—even in the fairy tale.

And there are the didactic plays which aim to inform. What are the children like in other parts of the Union? *Aul Gedzhe,* animated geography in good theatre form, recording Shestakov's travels along the borders of Asia, is the answer. What were the Tzars like? *The Pearl of Adalmina* replied, not too successfully, in visualized history. How did the boys and girls learn their lessons under the imperial régime? The curtain rises on a vivid drama of public school life during the Civil War called *The Wandering School*. What is the world like outside the U. S. S. R.? There is vigorous fantastic explanation in the operetta *We Are Strength*, in which daring and adventurous Young Pioneers tour the globe. The same question is more vehemently and unfairly answered in *The Brothers*, which belligerently contrasts life in the Union with life in France, to the disadvantage of France. This is a fine play dramatically, but its excellence is unpleasantly tarnished by an overdose of communistic propaganda, which might still be less a blemish had the playwright more regard for fair play.

Very different in style and purpose from these informatory plays are *The Squealer* and *Dzuba*, which demonstrate in clear theatrical idiom the ethical ideal for the young communist spectator. American audiences might be intrigued by *The Squealer* because it presents a nice problem which often arises in the schools of this country. "Don't be a tattle-tale" has always been a slogan among boys and girls. The Soviet attack is rather original: to be true to the people, one must not protect the individual against the people. Galsworthy in *Loyalties* wrestles with class and mass devotion, and, in that particular play, with personal justice.

The Squealer opens its curtain upon a group of the reclaimed wild boys of Moscow—those homeless vagabonds, products of the privation and suffering of the Civil War. For a long time these orphaned gamins eked out life beyond the pale of law. Their minds were warped to anti-social standards and nihilistic attitudes, although their sense of loyalty and responsibility to each other grew more keen. Reclaimed for normal life, a number of them are learning a useful trade in a shoe factory. There is a thief in the group. The boys know who he is, but true to each other, they rebel at being tattlers. The solution of the play emphasizes the importance of loyalty to common good—in this case the factory—before private or personal friendship. Good citizens must place the social order first. The child must learn the difference between the desirability of a guarded tongue in private affairs and a ready one in the service of the Commune.

Dzuba, Natalia Satz's highly amusing play, tells the children a tale of a little boy who wants to be different, a boy who is neither good nor bad, but who, chock full of nervous energy and imagination, keeps everything in a whirl. The presentation is most intriguing for the young audience, because the author never openly states when Dzuba is in the right or in the wrong, but so directs the children's minds that they are forced to figure out the answer for themselves. Dzuba's real name is Vassya. He lives in a world of his own creation where he crowns himself king of the make-believe land, Pashukanya. Everyday life in Pashukanya moves in the most extraordinary fashion. Smoke unscientifically floats down instead of up; the houses are built on the top of the chimneys; water flows out of table legs; and pants are worn for shirts and shirts for pants. Dzuba, becoming tired of his topsy-turvy realm, decides to go wandering, and inveigles his little playmate Ninka to take a trip about Moscow with him. They discover through many adventures that they are not like the rest and that being odd and queer is not always the best way to have fun—the ideal of mass consciousness versus individualism.

The morning after the first performance of *Dzuba,* Izvestia said: "The play solves the problem of how the fantastic is to be presented in the children's theatres. No nonsense. Everything is real." The unreality with which the play is filled is always in the youngsters' minds, not in their surroundings. It is a new type of fairy tale which gives free play to the imagination, but never permits the giant in *Jack and the Beanstalk* to become confused with the people of the material world. To point the transition from the real to the imaginary more vividly, the settings here represent a background of nature and there the false world which Vassya has manufactured. A novel scheme of cinema and live actors playing simultaneously has been perfected in this twofold responsibility of stage-craft. Animated cartoons of a Moscow street appear in one scene in which a street car comes tearing down upon the children, who sit placidly upon the rails. Vassya concocts the idea the passengers will be so grateful to have him and Ninka get off the tracks that costly gifts will be theirs when they permit the tram to pass. Of course, Dzuba didn't know that he had picked out the wrong track, and the cartoon train whizzes by them—no gifts, no accident, laughter from the surprised audience. Through this combination stagecraft, the theatrical intensity of the moment is realized and at the same time avoids too much naturalism which readily might be over-stimulating for the eight-to-ten-year-olds for whom the play is devised. "Suit the play to the children" is the plan.

To perform these plays of the children's theatre requires especially competent actors. They must be able to sing and dance as well as act. Above all they must be able to impersonate children, a task indeed. The success with which these players do this has won for them universal praise. Again and again visitors to the children's theatres refuse to believe that the characters represented on the stage are not youngsters. "How do you manage to do it so perfectly?" one visitor asked after a performance. "I have three of my own; I study them; I love them and I love my work; perhaps that helps me," replied the talented actress. The social responsibility of the actor is more clearly defined in the children's theatres than in the great playhouses of the Union.

Can there be a Proletarian Culture? Can art be democratic without playing down to the crowd? Can the masses be educated to the ideal of "our" theatre? The Union's answer is: "Yes, if the children are started in the right way." "How wonderful it is to see here that children are taught to love the theatre from the earliest age," remarked the French critic Mauprey, after attending his first performance for young spectators in Moscow. Art can be a very subtle weapon. Natalia Satz and her loyal followers have found a royal way to learning through the art of the Children's Theatres.

THE MUSICAL PLAY AND THE BALLET

IV

The Musical Play and the Ballet

HE DEMARCATION BETWEEN the spoken drama and the play with music is less clearly defined in Eastern Europe than in America. Opera and ballet in the Soviet Union are an integral part of everyday theatre experience; they are not neatly tucked into pigeonholes apart from the stage and catalogued as elaborate forms of program music or oratorio. The mighty achievements of the musical drama as a unit of theatre under the Imperialistic Russian Government were known the world round and are still pleasant in the memory of those who recall the days before the World War. "Have the excellencies of the tradition been lost?" "Has this new proletarian state cleared from the boards all that glorious operatic tradition?" These are questions frequently heard.

The answer is direct and simple. Water will flow over a dam. Time moves on, and life changes in the Union as elsewhere. The excellencies of old Russian opera and ballet, however, have not been lost; but an important corollary must be added—the musical drama has not been static during the last two decades. The Marinsky and Bolshoi are, obviously, no longer the opera houses of the Imperial Court; the ballet is no longer the leisurely pastime of a pleasure-bent nobility or of a complacent, sophisticated intelligentsia, but, for all that, these famous temples of the musical drama are still crowded with enthusiastic spectators, who represent not a class but a cross-section of contemporary Soviet life. In the new theatre, music becomes the possession of the many, not the few. Opera and ballet from the start were important items in the program for Proletarian Culture.

The audience for opera and ballet has changed. The musical drama itself has likewise changed. New theories have developed, and although the high standard of the old tradition is respected and preserved in composition and production, the musical plays have forged out their own destinies with cheerful, creative initiative. Novel methods of staging, of interpretation, of musical philosophy have developed. Outworn fashions have been discarded; many experiments have already been cast aside as foolish or unsatisfactory. Often widely admired successes are considered only moderately acceptable by the critical central committees. The stand-

ard of excellence is still as rigorous as it was in the days of the Tzars.
While general interest in opera wanes in Paris, New York, and London—
Leningrad, Moscow, Karkov, Kiev, and Baku find increasing audiences
clamoring at the doors. The Soviet musical drama is alive and popular.

Russian opera of the past and the Soviet opera of the present find one
common inspirational personality, who, unexpectedly, is not a musician
but a poet. It is almost impossible to discuss this musical drama without
making a bow to Pushkin. His influence in the past upon Glinka, Cui,
Mussorgski, Rimski, Asafiev, and Chaikovski is too well known to bear
repetition. The perennial demand for *Russlan and Ludmilla, Eugene
Onegin, The Fountain of Bakhchisarai, Coq d'or, Tzar Sultan, Boris
Godunov, Aleko,* and *Marva* bear vigorous testimony to his contemporary
popularity. That new arrangements of his old libretti are often made, and
that his poems are ever the source for new compositions attest his continued
influence. It has been said that Pushkin is a vital example of the common
sources of poetry and music. Surely the Soviet opera and ballet continue
to corroborate this statement.

Due to Pushkin, the Slavophils, and natural temperament, the old
musical drama was markedly nationalistic in character. The new opera
and ballet exhibit little deviation from the well trod route; nor is this
strange. The new régime inherits the spirit of an older art and adds thereto
its new philosophy, which, as yet, is far from being accepted outside the
borders of the Union. Naturally the new musical drama continues to
develop in thought and feeling within circumscribed geographical limits.
Although the rediscovery of the national minorities has brought new blood
to older traditions, the main strain of Soviet opera and ballet flows
unchanged. Nationalistic the musical drama was, and, for the present at
least, nationalistic it will remain.

The flares of the Revolution temporarily illuminated bypaths and
tortuous side streets. A wild desire to eliminate the old and to create
something entirely new was in the air. There was a pathetic but heroic
note in the devoted way composers, librettists, and choreographers burnt
themselves out vainly searching to find an untried method of expression
which would sweep clean the memory of the middle-class régime. How
history repeats and repeats! The Terror with its insane ardor tried in a like
manner to forget the civilization of the Grand Monarch. During the World
War, America tried to forget Wagner by darkening the Metropolitan for
a period to *Lohengrin* and *The Meistersingers.*

The months which followed breathlessly upon the October Days were
quite naturally a mêlée of restless inconsistencies. Texts were torn into

shreds and reconstructed nearer to a heart's desire which substituted revolutionary muck of banal content for the original libretto. Scenery was junked and replaced, as in the legitimate theatre, by wild constructivist nightmares which feebly purported "to express the machine." Prokoviev's *Love of Three Oranges* took on a Ringling Brothers atmosphere when it was performed by an ensemble of a hundred acrobats. The score was cut and slashed to match the swing of the rope ladders and trapezes. Atonality, dynamo music, even the invention of peculiar instruments to produce machine sound, the excessive use of quarter tones in scores — all these absurd experiments seemed temporarily the open road to a liberated opera and ballet. Strangely enough in these muddled days, the note of Scriabin's influence was distinctly heard again and again, like a trumpet sounding retreat from a battle where confusion marshaled her armies.

Apart from the outward struggle, there was a philosophic war forward on the field of theory. The goal was music for the masses, but the cause was not won with the turn of the hand. It became more and more obvious that the highly specialized music inspired by the physics laboratory, interesting escape as it was from the abhorred bourgeois Western tonal systems, was not readily comprehended by the people. Expressionism and scale trickery are not the simplest diet upon which to fatten a hungry Proletarian Culture. As a counter-force to these pitiful abstractions, Beethoven and Moussorgsky grew in favor and became the accepted models for a spell. Then the pendulum, pushed a bit by the Russian Association of Proletarian Musicians, which was composed of rabid reformers, began to swing too far the other way. This group was over-zealous in its desire to create proper Marxian music for the masses. Its fear and hatred of the bourgeois led it to doubt the harmlessness of the pastoral second act of *Eugene Onegin*, derived out of Chaikovski and Pushkin though it is. Such dictatorial control of operatic composition was perhaps more deadening to inspiration and creation than was the uncontrolled adoration of the machine which had preceded it. A new era of liberalism came into being when the Central Committee dissolved the Association in 1932.

While this war between theorists and ideologists continued, other forces were at work, attempting more sanely to discover acceptable revolutionary methods for writing and producing musical drama. Two familiar figures were introducing startling innovations in the operatic sphere. Through these changes, new courses of composition were being suggested which would be modern, reasonable, and, at the same time, capture the spirit of this elusive proletarian music. These men did not appear on the scene with a bundle of tricks from the scene-docks of the Bolshoi or the Marinsky.

They came from a dramatic theatre, the Moscow Art, and needed then, as now, no introduction. Stanislavsky and Danchenko have conducted their laboratory experiments in Moscow in two separate musical studios bearing their names. They started to revamp opera from scratch, and hit, as their first point of attack, at the artificial absurdities of the grand tradition.

The musical world has long recognized that opera is in far too many productions a hybrid thing which is often neither musical nor dramatic. Wagner saw this difficulty clearly and tried to improve, with noteworthy success, the maladjustment of the factors which make up an opera. In spite of his courageous innovations, opera frequently continues to fall between the horns of a dilemma. The libretto hampers the music, or the score slows down the action. Conductors as a lot have paid little attention to correcting this fault. With few exceptions, they have been so utterly engrossed in the music as pure music that the drama has fuddled along and filled in a gap here and there as best it could. The convention of opera has accepted accomplished vocal interpretation at the expense of adequate acting, some-times permitting the vocalization to stand the test with no support from histrionics whatsoever.

Stanislavsky began with the idea that it is possible to sing and act at the same time. This is not an arresting thought, nor is it startlingly original or novel. Mary Garden always believed in the actor-singer and exemplified her belief in her performances. Stanislavsky, however, has carried the hypothesis to a more conclusive end than any of his predecessors. He has dreamed, first, that opera can be made plausible. To materialize this dream he has applied all the resources and paraphernalia of his complicated naturalistic creed to the musical play. He has sweat blood attempting to limber up the action, temper the characterization with reasonable psy-chology, embrace the ensemble as an integral part of the story, blend the interpretation of the score with the action and character. His results fascinate the most stubborn conventionalists in the musical world, even though some of his productions may not be regarded as overwhelming successes.

His scholarly, detailed production of *Eugene Onegin*, partly because the libretto of Pushkin and the music of Chaikovski naturally synthesize, is generally considered a triumphant venture with the singing actor. His *Carmen* justly could be called a greater success, because the task of unifica-tion is far more difficult. Carmen, under the inspiration of his thoughtful direction, does suggest a flesh and blood gypsy. The stagy story is tinted with a hue of possibility and sincere human passion. Dramatically there can be no doubt that the play becomes a real play. To those trained to hear

Bizet sung in the Metropolitan or Parisian manner, the score may sound muffled and suppressed. The musical heroics have vanished, and extreme simplicity has replaced bombast. Of course, that is precisely what Stanislavsky set out to accomplish. He fills the eye first, the ear afterwards. One *watches* his *Carmen* with greater interest than one listens. He has created theatre and not concert.

Nemirovitch-Danchenko is more daring than his colleague. He hopes to create an entirely new type of musical drama which will harmoniously unite all of the possibilities known to the theatre. Libretto, score, acting, singing, *mise en scène,* and *décor* all share equally in his scheme to bring a richer experience to the audience. Wagner also had such a plan in mind. To accomplish this Danchenko vaguely gropes to find the underlying tonal thought and philosophic rhythm of the play. His theory may be vague, but his practice is concrete indeed. He sometimes finds it expedient, as in his adaptation of *Carmen,* which American audiences may have seen a few years ago, to discard the existing libretto and write a new one, which, as he contends, will strain the score less and will portray more objectively the "inner soul" of music and story.

To realize this aim he calls the theatre of Dionysus to his aid. In *Lysistrata* and *La Traviata* the members of the chorus are brought to the foreground not as a conventional ensemble, but as a mass commentator upon the action. In *Carmen* the Greek influence is more apparent still. On a bridge above the actor-singers, the chorus sit like majestic Fates permitting no movement on the stage to pass by their all-seeing eyes without appropriate reaction timed with the musical notation or, more impressively, recorded in the ominous flutter of their huge Spanish fans. The effect is striking. *Carmen* as a fate tragedy is "new opera" indeed. The audience is forced into consciousness of the power of Danchenko's keen sense of theatre which stands him in good use while he blazes the trail for the musical drama of tomorrow.

The precise effect which Stanislavsky and Danchenko will have upon the future of opera and ballet is uncertain. It is presumptuous to entertain the thought that musical drama will be completely revolutionized by the enthusiasms of these ardent and sincere pioneers. If, however, they succeed in destroying within the Soviet Union alone an opera cult hidebound in nineteenth century forms, in reconstructing it in terms of better theatre, and in creating a less hybrid art, their efforts will not have been wasted. If singers can be taught to portray character as well as produce tone, if conductors can be schooled to remember the libretto and the score in their interpretation, if composers, above all, can be bred to blend the philosophy of music with the philosophy of theatre action and life, a millennium in music drama is at hand. The Union is confident that the new theatre is already doing these things, and points with pride at some of its more spectacular achievements.

To change the course of production is one thing, but to discover a new musical philosophy is quite another. It is difficult to understand music of revolution. The leftist does not always seem able to explain himself without a torrent of language which often results in confusion. One can grasp fairly easily the conflict which the Marxian art feels with mystical philosophy, the oversentimental, and the supermelodic which borders on prettiness. If such elements are counter-revolutionary and middle-class to the Marxians, these qualities must be eliminated from the opera and ballet in a socialistic state. Beyond this issue, however, the course of thought becomes less and less obvious. Music has, certainly, an expressive language of its own and a philosophy which is its peculiar possession; but its speech is abstract. To assume that C is revolutionary and that C+ is anti-socialistic might appear to some as begging the question. The more pessimistic might predict that to create a revolutionary opera and ballet, the Soviet Union will be forced, at length, to depend upon the libretto and its message and be content if musical notes, without exhibiting any especial Marxian significance, synchronize reasonably with the words.

To attain a revolutionary musical drama by means of libretto has already been tried. New ballets and operas based on socialistic subject-matter have been compiled in generous numbers. The bulk of these are the work of comparatively young composers. Several names known in Tzarist days, however, do pop up in the list. Serge Vassilenko has contributed an opera, *The Son of the Sun*. Andrei Pashchenko has turned the historical episode of Pugachev's revolt into a musical drama entitled *The Eagle's Rebellion*. Leo Knipper's *North Wind*, adapted from Kirschon's play *The City of High Winds*, deals with the tragic death of the Commissars at Baku and is accredited the position of being one of the first Soviet operas dealing with a contemporary subject. More distinguished than these on the roll-call of the older generation is Boris Asafiev, who composed the much admired Soviet ballet, *The Flames of Paris*. His contemporary, Reingold Gliere, born a Belgian, wrote *The Red Poppy* and was commissioned by the Turkoman Minority Opera to provide a score for *Shah-Senem*, the libretto for which is based upon native Turkish legends.

Asafiev's *The Flames of Paris* utilizes with considerable ingenuity as themes for its score the revolutionary songs of the French Terror and the Commune. The Soviet critics claim that the choreography in this ballet has with more than adequate success freed itself from "the dead weight of old traditions" and that "signal advances have been made upon all the previous ballets." Neither the libretto nor the score is at any point unusual.

The libretto is jammed and crammed to the point of bulging with melodramatic scenes. A child in a hamlet near Marseilles is ridden down by the huntsmen from the château in a fashion that parallels the episode of the Marquis's coach in *The Tale of Two Cities*. The château is stormed by the angry peasants; a performance of *Armida* is interrupted by the Revolutionaries in Paris; the Tuileries is sacked, and the people celebrate their victory to the tune of the *Marseillaise;* the cry "Labor and peace for the people" frantically rings out when the tri-color triumphs. *The Flames of Paris* provides a moving spectacle wherein action and music complement each other.

This historical ballet of the past is rivaled in popular favor by one from the present. *The Red Poppy* tells the story of a Chinese maiden who falls in love with an officer of the Red Army. The sinister forces opposing Bolshevism in the Orient are at work, aided by the British Government. The foreign commander of the troops of intervention plots in melodramatic fashion to murder the Red Officer by poisoning him. Loyal to her love, the Chinese girl risks life itself to defeat her lover's foes. She succeeds in saving her Red Army hero, but a bullet finds her a mark. As she is dying, her eyes are fixed upon a red poppy. To the Communist audience the ballet is probably a symbol of China's wistful longing to cast her lot with the U. S. S. R., but which may not be because of the capitalistic policy in the Far East. With or without the interpretation, the emotional note strikes to the heart without resorting to sentimentality. The score interprets the spirit of the story, but can hardly claim distinction.

Themes of old rebellion and modern international crisis augment the repertory of the contemporary librettist. Satire steadily gains a more important place. Years ago Rimski-Korsakov, abetted by Pushkin, found the power of humorous criticism ready material for opera, and the result was *Coq d'or*. It may be that this opera-ballet is the suggestive force which has influenced modern Soviet composers to walk the paths of satire. It is also possible that a philosophy which denies the mystical and wages war upon the sentimental has been influential in directing the steps of the musical play along these paths. Borodine's burlesque opera *Heroes* pokes fun at the conventions of Verdi, Gounod, and Strauss, and—like Shaw in *Fanny's First Play*—also burlesques himself. Lampooning to musical accompaniment can be a most telling weapon in the theatre. Gilbert and

Sullivan knew its value; Kaufman and Hart have not neglected their tradition.

A popular ballet in the satiric style is *The Three Fat Men,* arranged from a novel and play by Olesha and set to music by Oranski. Once upon a time there was an unhappy land ruled over by three aristocratic and tyrannical fat men. A revolutionist, Prospero, harangued the workers to action and led them in an attack against the palace, but loyal guards frustrated the revolt, and Prospero was thrown into a dungeon cell. During the celebration or imperial orgy which followed, Prince Tutti's lifelike doll was broken. The Prince, a pampered son of wealth, was in a state of collapse because of this heartrending misfortune. Nothing could divert him, or dry his tears. At length a learned doctor was discovered who agreed to call all science to aid in repairing the damaged puppet, but unfortunately he mislaid his valuable patient at a village fair. His despair was checked, however, by the appearance of a traveling theatrical company which had among its members a marvelously beautiful woman. This leading lady agreed to impersonate the doll. She was introduced into the palace by the doctor. Tutti was very happy to have his plaything so miraculously repaired, and began to dance madly with her. Weakling that he was, he became completely worn out by so much exercise and fell into a coma or sleep. The actress seized this rare opportunity to steal the dungeon key from her fatigued lover. Of course, she freed Prospero, who this time led the willing laborers to victory against the guards of the three fat men. The masses won and there was general rejoicing in the village. The ballet was first produced by a young choreographer, Moiseyev, who, rode to fame on the great popularity of the piece in Moscow and Leningrad.

The marked favor which a satiric ballet like *The Three Fat Men* finds with a proletarian audience is possibly explained by the obvious burlesque of a capitalistic state and the trenchant thrusts at the mental and physical weakness of aristocratic Prince Tutti. Then, too, the libretto gives a backhanded compliment to the toiler. But such superficial explanations do not account for the deep-seated love of the dance in the Slavic temperament, which predilection has been known through the centuries and has not been developed suddenly in these days of mass culture. New compositions, whatever their nature, find formidable competitors in the classical repertory. *The Fountains of Bakhchisarai, The Sleeping Beauty,* and *Prince Igor* regularly delight the audiences in the Metropolitan centers.

The more philosophic ballets, which interpret musical abstractions, are not so often represented in the Union as those which tell a story. Critics there are who on this ground challenge the appreciative depth of the mass audience. "Anybody can follow a story," they sigh. And in the spirit of a *non sequitur* they add with finality, "The days of Nijinsky are gone forever." There is no doubt that a stirring plot is easier to follow than an æsthetic abstraction. No one can deny that the glories of the ballet when Pavlova and Mordkin graced the boards of the Marinski would be hard to equal. Yet the inherent love of the dance vigorously asserts itself in growing Soviet audiences, and the artists continue to emulate the technical excellencies which the world applauded under the old régime.

While some new composers have been devoting themselves to ballet, others have been concerned with the exacting process of creating opera. Many new scores have been performed. Sometimes the composers have turned to foreign countries for their libretti as was the case with Polovenkin's version of *The Playboy of the Western World*. The usual policy has been, however, to encourage the use of native material and to follow the nationalistic spirit of the Slavophils. In an attempt to create a socialistic opera, the themes of the Revolution and Civil War have been repeatedly brought to the stage by the younger men. There has been no shortage of premières in the Union during the last ten years even if theme material has been curtailed.

Two post-Tzarist composers have gained recognition both at home and abroad. They are Dmitri Shostakovitch and Ivan Dzerzhinsky. Dzerzhinsky was about ten years old when the Revolution broke in fury. At twenty-seven he had experienced the thrill of seeing his first opera produced in Moscow and Leningrad and had been honored by receiving the special commendation of Stalin. *Quiet Flows the Don* dramatizes for its libretto the widely read novel by Sholokov. Peasant life along the placid river in the days before the holocaust of world strife swept the valley is represented in the opening scenes. The call to arms separates youthful lovers. The dreary hours of war wear on. Nobles indulge in violence and seduction while the laborers are fighting at the front. The locale shifts to a tired and discouraged Russian army camp. The soldiers mutiny. The Revolution wipes out all old scores in a baptism of fire and blood, bringing a new day and a new opportunity for all.

The libretto is staccato in its technique. Taken as a whole, the opera presents a cold, hard review of peasant existence in an outworn civilization and a happy release from the past through revolt. If the music is not unusual or distinguished, at least the score does not interfere with the feverish, violent onrush of the story. The applause for his first attempt had hardly died out when Dzerzhinsky's second opera, *The Soil Upturned*, was performed in Moscow and repeated the success of *Quiet Flows the Don*.

The Union believes that this young man has promise and that he is well on his way in creating a true proletarian opera which will join music and social purpose in perfect union. Time will tell.

Time has dealt harshly with Dmitri Shostakovitch. The day is not long since he was toasted as the composer of a new opera, and *Katerina Ismailova,* known in America as *Lady Macbeth of Mtsensk,* was heralded as the most brilliant of modern musical productions. Shostakovitch says of himself: "I am striving to create my own musical language, which I endeavor to make simple and expressive. I cannot imagine my own further development otherwise than connected with our own socialist construction. And the aim which I have put before myself is with my musical creations to help as far as lies within my power in the building up of our wonderful country. There can be no greater joy for a composer than the knowledge that by his creation he is furthering the progress of Soviet musical culture, which will play a prominent rôle in the reshaping of the human mind."

Katerina Ismailova resurrects the life of the merchant class in old Tzarist Russia. The story which the libretto describes is a thoroughly unpleasant one: faithlessness, murder, and finally suicide. When the opera was pro- duced in 1933, Soviet critics agreed that the composer, who was able to recreate the past in terms of contemporary socialistic idealism, was making an invaluable contribution to the growth of a Proletarian Culture, and that Shostakovitch's *Katerina* was "the biggest landmark in the development of opera." Three years later *Pravda* denounced the same opera as "a product of petty bourgeois formalism and insincere and unnecessary trickery." His ballet, *Limpid Stream,* which deals with the farm collective, was considered coarse and stylized. Does such a change of heart indicate fickleness in criticism, disfavor with a star chamber, or is a new epoch in the progress of music for the masses at hand? In America his melodic passages are likely to linger pleasantly in the memory even though the thunder of new ideologies drowns his song at home. That he is not discouraged is evidenced by his recently contributed musical setting for the superfilm *The Return of Maxim.*

One of the key-notes of the Soviet Union is to accept and to profit by constructive criticism. This is a particularly salutary philosophy for a nation busy with experimentation. The younger composers find their days well filled as they seek to discover new and less artificial forms of musical drama, to carry the spirit of production suggested by the Moscow musical studios into the core of composition. A new world is in the making, and they are sincerely anxious to give full measure of service to extending the borders of Proletarian Culture. Their efforts already are rewarded with

some success. They have good reason to feel encouraged, for the conventional routines which have shackled opera are being broken by their realistic
attacks. New scores are composed with nervous speed and are produced
with painstaking care.

Sharing an important place with the experimental, the dignified classical
repertory of Rimsky and Chaikovski gives balance and stability to the
contemporary programs. Imaginative and occasionally startling new productions of tried favorites are everyday occurrences within the Union.
In addition to the traditional source materials, the national minorities are
contributing their folklore to the librettists, their songs to the composers,
and their dances to the choreographers. The music drama, old and new, is
essentially alive. Its leaders are not afraid to admit their mistakes, and rise
upon the stepping-stones of their corrected errors. The Soviet opera
and ballet neither slumber nor sleep.

Can the masses sincerely enjoy opera? A brief season in New York and
London appears sufficient to satisfy the demands of a diamond horseshoe,
but five Grand Opera Houses playing ten months a year cannot satisfy the
demands in Moscow. There is a Soviet slogan which runs, "Music is as
essential to us as bread." Proletarian Culture is no dream when the *Theatre
at the Left* raises its curtain upon its musical drama.

OLD WINE IN NEW BOTTLES

OLD WINE IN NEW BOTTLES

V

Old Wine in New Bottles

ENIN URGED THE Revolution to seek broader understanding through the culture of the past. He further advised that only through the study of older civilizations and the assimilation of their excellencies could a proletarian state lay its foundation upon solid ground. In the new theatre old playwrights share the scene with contemporaries: Shakspere rubs shoulders with Pogodin, Molière with Slavin, and Chekhov with Kirschon. The energetic, self-conscious endeavor of the Division of Education to follow the counsel of the leader explains readily enough why playing the classics, native and foreign, forms such an important item in the Soviet repertory.

The classics have a special social function in the new theatre. The contemporary playwright and audience may grow in critical appreciation through active association with the best stage craftsmanship the old world has produced these two thousand years. Through first-hand knowledge of the drama, the Soviet stage believes its artistic standards can be raised. In the fine arts, the communistic ideology, assuming the rôle of liberality, finds importance, not only in mastering the Marxian creed, but in keeping on speaking terms at least with the course of bourgeois philosophy. To appreciate the brilliance of the sun by observing its shadow; to reinterpret the human relationships represented in the older playwright in the spirit of his own day and to correlate that interpretation with the present; to penetrate beyond the confines of period and epoch and relate the play and its maker to the procession of civilization as a whole—these are a few of the weighty purposes through which the new theatre brings a renaissance to the standard drama.

For example, the new theatre might study *Othello* to discover how Shakspere built his scenes, how he created his dramatic effects, and how he molded his characters. Its interest might be focused on the bourgeois philosophy represented by parental and civil authority, by the color of the Moor, by the femininity of Desdemona. The race problem presented by Othello would certainly be considered stimulating, first from the Elizabethan and modern English point of view, and, second, from the more liberal outlook of the U. S. S. R. Again, *Othello* might be worth the two hours' traffic of the stage as an abstract study of the motives of jealousy and prejudice. In a like manner, the Soviet theatre would labor to unearth something old and something new in *The Bourgeois Gentil-homme, Kabale und Liebe, The Inspector General*, or *The Storm*. After this pressing-out process of comparisons and contrasts, the usual academic classroom residue of dramatic literature is rediscovered, with this important addition: in the Soviet Union, the residue is decanted to life in the theatre rather than allowed to dry in the cask of pedantic archives. The theatre is classless. If the results of scholarly labor are good, learning's benefits are good for the masses to share. The Union is very sure of its course. The old wine is in new bottles.

The new theatre has, however, a spontaneous as well as an academic enthusiasm for standard drama. There is nothing apologetic about a per-formance of Ostrovski in Moscow. There is nothing of conventional respect exhibited toward a performance of Fonvizin, Griboyedov, or Gogol any-where in the Soviet Republic. In the Union the classics are not sacrosanct or even sacred, certainly not "socially proper;" they are useful and interesting. They are current coin of the realm, not show-case coppers of a dead civilization. One learns to love the best theatre by familiarity with the high-water-marks of stage history.

The dominating figure in the national classic repertory is Alexander Ostrovski, who lived during the middle years of the nineteenth century. He could have remembered the first night of Lytton's *Richelieu*; he lived long enough to have seen Ibsen's *Ghosts*. He was a contemporary of the renowned school of Russian realists — Tolstoi, Dostoyevski, Turgenev — and, without doubt, he was influenced by them, or at least shared with them the fervor of the naturalist movement. He wrote over fifty plays, many of which met with considerable success in his own day; others suffered the censorship of the Imperial Régime and were not honored in public representation until after his death. Besides writing plays, he was tireless and persistent in his struggle to interest the government in establishing state playhouses. His moderate success in his own day has now been realized fifty-and a hundredfold. The cliché—"before his time"—is proved true again.

Today, if he is to be judged by the frequency with which his plays are presented, Ostrovski is the most popular playwright in the repertory of the new theatre, but this loyal devotion of the masses cannot be entirely due to the skill or excellence of his dramaturgy, which is scarred by careless faults and blemishes. Like most of the naturalists, he is a master of minute details which, crowding the scene, warp the proportion and shrink the effectiveness. The structure, as a result, becomes loose and flabby and disproportioned. Here, the colorful dialogue swallows the plot; there, conclusions and resolutions are shockingly abrupt, and the final curtain falls upon an unconvincing scene. Ostrovski fails to meet the requirements of a first-rate technician. This is indeed a pity, for his influence, conscious or unconscious, upon the writing of young Soviet playwrights is tremendous. As a model, he is partly responsible for the careless craftsmanship of many of the contemporary dramatic writers.

But this very failing is, in a sense, his own greatest strength. The careless ease with which he reproduces lifelike bits must be admired. He holds the mirror up to life and catches the perfect and often repulsive reflection of the Romanov merchant class. Like Ibsen, he is a man of the theatre first and a reformer incidentally. He is also a satirist whose well directed darts against the decadent idealism of the sixties and the self-satisfied hypocrisy of the Moscow bourgeoisie have, reasonably, endeared him to the new theatre and the proletarian state. His characters cry out for interpretation. Actors are ever happy to be cast in his plays. Audiences are ever happy to watch the casts in action. He is the heart of the national classic tradition.

Ostrovski is always in the repertory of the more important state theatres. In Moscow in 1936 his plays were represented in over seventeen different productions, which included *Wolves and Sheep, Mad Money, Talents and Admirers, The Forest, Poverty is No Crime, A Warm Heart, No Accounts Needed*, and *The Storm. Poverty is No Crime, The Forest*, and *Mad Money* are usually considered his best plays. In the same season there were productions of Fonvizin's timeless satire on education, *The Minor*. Gogol was represented by *Marriage, Dead Souls*, and the internationally admired *Revizor*. Tolstoi's *Resurrection, Anna Karenina*, and *The Fruits of Knowledge* were popular as ever. Subhovo-Kobylin's *Kerchinski's Wedding* as usual was played. Chekhov, respected but held in lower esteem than formerly, was heard in the everlasting *Cherry Orchard, Vaudeville* (a series of one-acters), and *The Three Sisters*.

In addition to these plays from the old Russian régime, the foreign classics were well represented by Schiller's *Don Carlos* and *Kabale und Liebe;* de Vega's *The Gardener's Dog*, Calderon's *His Own Jailer*, Beaumarchais's *The Marriage of Figaro*, de Musset's *On ne badine pas avec l'amour*, Scribe's *Glass of Water, Adrienne Lecouvrier*, and *One Hand Washes the Other*. Dumas's *Camille*, Fletcher's *The Spanish Curate*, Gozzi's *Princess Turandot* were also popular; but Shakspere, as ever, held first place among the foreign writers. *Othello, Lear, Twelfth Night, Romeo and Juliet, The Merry Wives of Windsor*, and *Egyptian Nights* (*Antony and Cleopatra*) were the current favorites, some of these represented by two and three simultaneous productions. Perhaps New York and London are slipping. Must one go to Moscow to see Shakspere played?

A list is never more than a list, but in a poor way this schedule of the Russian and foreign classics produced in one theatrical center in one season will indicate the respectful attention which the Central Dramatic Committee pays the heritage of the past. One should remember, moreover, that the theatres of Leningrad, Karkov, Kiev, Odessa, and Baku, in a less pretentious way to be sure, present programs arranged on the Moscow plan. These play-lists certainly suggest that the new theatre is honestly interested in the great milestones of dramatic literature; that it believes these successful plays of other days have something to teach the present; that a proletarian culture grows in strength through assimilating the knowledge of past experience. Surely a winter in the Moscow theatres provides a comprehensive course in drama which any American college catalogue might envy. "Know your theatre, not through the library, but on the scene." But such a slogan is futile if the theatre does not provide the plays. The new theatre *does* provide. The masses *do* attend. The cultural program of the Soviet Union ever increases its sphere of influence.

"Does the new theatre distort the classics into propaganda pieces so mutilated that the average playgoer could never recognize the old favorites?" The Soviet theatre does believe, as has been suggested, that an "archæological approach" should be avoided. It is not primarily concerned with "museum-like restorations of dead-and-gone theatrical epochs." The chief motive behind production is to stress significant social relationships of the play with modern life. To realize this end, the Soviet stage allows itself a latitude of interpretation which is liberally unconventional, but which is nowise inconsistent with the basic meaning of the text.

Such free manœuvering of script might have been seen even at Stratford a year ago when Iden Payne produced *Troilus and Cressida* as an anti-war play. Some students can remember the distinguished American scholar who taught his Shakspere course each year with a fresh crop of personal prejudices; one entire semester was spent in a brilliant demonstration that Shakspere was an anti-Puritan propagandist. When *Hamlet* was produced by the Vakhtangov Theatre in Moscow as a satiric comedy, there was a storm of protest in the Union. An American scholar recently discovered with immoderate enthusiasm that *Julius Caesar* was a high comedy. Perhaps a storm of protest should have been raised in America. When Meyerhold took excessive liberties with *The Inspector General,* the Moscow critics were the first to rebel. The Soviet theatre does not tolerate warping the text. The new theatre *does* believe that the text should be interpreted in terms which will give it modern richness and contemporary social significance.

Then pops the question, "But doesn't the new theatre metamorphose all the stage into a communist propaganda forum?" Yes, and no. Once, to be sure, Fifth Avenue was an unpaved cowpath. In the early days of the Soviet régime, without doubt, the stage classics became instruments for mad and over-enthusiastic Revolutionists. The fear of counter-revolutionary thinking approached mania. Every muscle was strained to fight the proletarian battle. The results were dramatic monstrosities. At the present time there is no fanatical attempt to perform a miracle which increases a Marxian kernel to a bushel of communist wheat. As muddy paths of Fifth Avenue gave way to asphalt pavement, so too the defiant painting-the-classics-bright-red, common as it was in the early period of the Soviet theatre, has passed. That the theatre of the Union does see life communistically and not capitalistically is, of course, also natural and true. As the philosophies of the Western World differ from those of the Union, the theatrical interpretation of the classics is bound likewise to differ. New York sees *Othello* with capitalistic eyes; Moscow sees *Othello* through communistic lenses. This is not a calamity for either Broadway or the Red Square.

The most radical producer of the first two decades of the new theatre was Meyerhold. Since 1917 he has rehearsed, rewritten, and presented many plays of established reputation. Ostrovski's *Forest,* Dumas's *Camille,* Gogol's *Revizor,* and Griboyedov's *Woe to Wit* have been outstanding productions in his theatre. Because the very name of Meyerhold has always raised a storm of controversy, it is not surprising that his interpretations of the good old plays have been found shocking both within and without the Union. There was little of *Revizor* left, except the Gogol philosophy, after Meyerhold had set to work with his kit of tools. To which observation the genius director would doubtless have replied, if asked: "I didn't intend that there should be." The childlike exuberance with which he revised the masters reminds one strongly of the manhandling of standard plays and novels by the Hollywood Studios. It might be remembered also that Shaw presumes to improve Shakspere.

In *Woe to Wit,* decorated extravagantly with bizarre and eccentric stagecraft, he reproduced, nevertheless, a telling atmospheric cartoon of the Moscow decadents of the 1830's. The normal, natural impersonation of Chatski contrasted against the painted stylized figures of the gentry revealed with sharp accents the inner theatrical motives of the play. Though the superficial externals of Griboyedov's text were portrayed with

great inexactitude, surely the deeper purpose of the play was clearly
flashed upon the retina and hammered upon the eardrums of the audience.
Griboyedov's satire in Meyerhold's hands showed, by forcefully relating
this classic to modern life, a considerable gain over a purely historical,
archæological method.

Woe to Wit was one of Meyerhold's last experiments. There was a
marked change in this extremist director in the last decade. He became
more and more circumspect as the seasons turned. A comparison of *The
Forest,* produced incomprehensibly in 1923, with Woe to Wit is indicative
of the broad sweep of dramatic interpretation in the new theatre. Preserv-
ing the rights of self-expression and still maintaining a sense of daring and
progressiveness, the current playing of the classics has been freed from
former madness and hysteria. Lenin said nothing about a "*mis*"-understand-
ing of the culture of the past as an aid in building a proletarian state.

The method pursued in the recent restaging of Tolstoi's *Resurrection*
would perhaps carry more weight with the conservatives than would either
old or new productions by Meyerhold. The dramatization of this naturalistic novel of the last century has been well known in the theatres of
America for many years; the opera libretto, adapted from its pages,
provided Mary Garden with one of her most spectacular acting rôles.
When the Moscow Art Theatre director scanned the sheets of the old
script, he saw at once that the usual stage version missed a very important
turn in Tolstoi's book. The social philosophy for which he was so famous
had been wholly neglected in a feverish drive to tell the story with
theatrical force.

The stage play had made the famous court scene in the third act the
dramatic climax. After Raskolnikov had pondered over the revision of the
play for the new production, he decided to make this point of the novel his
opening act. The old version had stressed the downfall and degeneration
of Katusha; the new version stressed the rebirth of womanhood. To drama-
tize the philosophy of the play more deftly for the audience, the author is
made a member of the cast and mingles with the crowd. After the manner
of Hamlet at the play, he frequently halts the action to emphasize more
forcefully the situation. At moments he talks for the characters on the
scene, leaving to them the difficult task of a complicated pantomime. In
performance, these explanatory interpolations seem neither strange nor
unusual, for Raskolnikov's method lends the whole of theatre facilities to
the demands of the novel technique, never attempting to confine it within
the mechanical routine of a well-made Scribian play. By his production

of *Resurrection* Tolstoi is restored, and a much needed new technique of novel dramatization is introduced.

One tremendously effective scene deserves special comment. After the trial at which Prince Dimitre has recognized the woman on the stand as the girl whom he had seduced years before, he returns home. In his study he paces backward and forward for a long time. His thoughts are upon the events of the day. His seared conscience is beginning to speak to him again for the first time since his youth. The scene lasts a good fifteen minutes; Prince Dimitre, played to a turn by Erchov, says never a word. At intervals the eloquent silence is broken by the player-author, who, from the audience side of the footlights, with telling tragic force comments upon the battle within the mind of the young noble. In its new interpretation *Resurrection* has become almost as great in the theatre as it is in the bound pages of Tolstoi's novel. In its new interpretation, the lurid and exciting melodrama of old Russia becomes a compelling, gripping psychological study of yesterday and today as well.

Encouraged by its success with *Resurrection,* the Gorki Art Theatre has tried to provide another more faithful and exact representation of Tolstoi for the people in a new production of *Anna Karenina* which does not deny the overpowering force of "bourgeois" love. Through this same progressive spirit of dramatization, Gogol's *Dead Souls,* a harsh and horrid picture of the Russian landowner of the old régime, assumes a position in the repertory almost as important as that so long enjoyed by the established *Inspector General.* It might be asserted that this ever ambitious body of thoughtful artists has found a striking method of transferring the novel from the library to the stage without subjecting it to the hampering restrictions of technique. Raskolnikov shares honors, at any rate in this particular field, with Bryan Doherty, Thomas Jones, and Helen Jerome.

If Meyerhold at times wandered far away from the text to come nearer, as he believed, to the inner meaning of the play, the Gorki Art Theatre with its intimate realistic methods has given Tolstoi and Gogol fresh vigor by representing upon the scene for the first time, as they contend, the true intent of the author. The Vakhtangov productions of Gozzi's *Princess Turandot* and of *Hamlet* lean toward the Meyerhold scheme. With the Italian classic that theatre was extremely successful; with the British masterpiece, less happy. Hamlet, strutting the boards as a satiric comedy prince, makes the average Anglo-Saxon mind hope that this is a nightmare and that the crowing of the cock will usher in a normal dawn. The universal difference of opinion surrounding this elusive Dane can hardly include justification for the Vakhtangov extravagance. Insult couples with injury when Ophelia's madness finds a stark substitute in delirium tremens. That the Soviet theatre world was annoyed by these absurd liberties of interpretation, which seemed to border on flat burlesque, reëchoes the displeasure which it expressed with Meyerhold's *Revizor*. The new theatre would not confuse freedom of interpretation with annihilation of the author.

In contrast to the Vakhtangov *Hamlet*, Radlov produces *Othello* with academic loyalty to text, except for the Bianca episodes, which are generously padded. Whatever germ of a race problem there may be in the play comes to the fore with this skillful *regisseur* in charge. The character of the Moor glows with more startling Oriental color than is usual in the English-American theatre. At the Krassnaya-Pressnya, Okhlopkov sets the same play in unique fashion, but tampers little, if at all, with its usual meaning. The Jewish State stages and interprets *Lear* with barbaric splendor, which has little to do with Holinshed but much to do with brilliant acting. The First Studio translates *Twelfth Night* into a stylized fantasy, lending the mistaken identities and the uncertain coastal survey of Illyria a new garment of truth and plausibility. *Kabale und Liebe,* well mounted by Akimov, melodramatically unearths a social kinship with the French Revolution which Schiller surely never dreamed of; but it is splitting hairs to worry about that, for the loveliness of the production warrants a few liberties. Shakspere, Schiller, Gozzi. The carefree manner in which the Soviet stage adapts these playwrights of other lands might cause the pedant to gasp, but the result (even *Hamlet*) is always good theatre which inclines the masses toward the giants of drama with friendliness in their hearts rather than driving them, filled with fear of the highbrow, away from these Promethean figures.

The repertory system of the new theatre attempts to make the classics accessible to the people through stage representation as well as through library stacks. The outcome is an interested audience of workers who sit elbow to elbow at the play just as they toil elbow to elbow at the machine— a united body which is proud to be on intimate terms with Gogol, Griboyedov, and Ostrovski, and which admires the craftsmanship of foreign genius from Sophocles to Shakspere and Schiller. One winter in Moscow alone offers opportunity to see more of the standard plays in performance than in any other theatrical capital in the world. This is a sweeping statement which is not disproved by the long and excellent tradition of the Comédie Française in Paris or by the crowded and well selected programs of the German subsidized stages.

The extent of the classic repertory of the Soviet Republic is phenomenal. The unconventional latitude of interpreting this repertory is intriguing and varied. The Lenin text has been applied to the theatre, and the masses are learning the error of the old belief that the best in art is highbrow and therefore not for the great unwashed. Hamlet, Chatski, Sganarelle, Katerina, Khlestakov, and Cleopatra are now the possessions of a classless society. The old wine has been rebottled once again. The theatre of the Soviet Union contributes its part to building a Proletarian Culture by playing the classics.

PLAYS BORN OF REVOLUTION

VI

Plays Born of Revolution

HEN THE HOUSES of Lancaster and York had settled their differences on Bosworth Field and the Tudors had established a new royal line; when, a little later, foreign intervention in English affairs came to a melodramatic conclusion in the spectacular destruction of the Spanish Armada, a nationalistic England became aware of her own strength and importance. Through the long reign of Elizabeth, the realm concerned itself with internal growth and the pursuit of peaceful arts. The time was ready for the poets, replacing soldiers, to sing commemoratively the romance of battles. Among these Shakspere was preeminently successful in recording the triumph of the ruling house. Lacking much as stage plays, these chronicle dramas proclaimed a mighty tribute to England and its Lady Queen.

A pertinent parallel is discernible between the Elizabethan historical dramas and the plays which filled the theatrical vacuum left by the Bolshevic Revolution. On one hand the February Days had been long in the making; on the other the overthrow of the corrupt Tzarist state was not the conclusion of strife, but, rather, the beginning of a dreary, bloody contest between the Whites and the Reds. In 1917 there were no roses as emblems. The Spanish crisis in England's destiny finds a counterpart in the wars of intervention which the new régime was compelled to wage against the foreign powers. When these chaotic hours were past, the fledgling Soviet Republic caught its spent breath and peered out above the ruins. The struggle had been sordid, but victory had come. The cause had won.

The playmakers came to the fore by hundreds with pens ready to write the costly trail of the *Sickle and Hammer* into romances for the ravenous theatre. The span of revolution from the execution of Stenka Razin to the moment when the last French soldier left Odessa bridged nearly four hundred years of battle for freedom. As Shakspere sang, so too Vishnevski, and Kirschon, and Slavin, and Ivanov sang. The impressive pageant of Communist history unfolded before the eyes of the people and became a highly-colored tapestry for the renovated stage. Plays of Prelude and Revolution, plays of Civil War and Intervention cheered in a gruff and

dissonant chorus the cause of fallen heroes and reveled in the consumma-
tion of the dictatorship of the Proletariat.

Among the themes of prelude, that of the daring Robin Hood of Russia,
Stenka Razin, is the most popular. This Cossack highwayman from 1667
to 1671 swept the Volga territory with his bandit followers, pillaging and
burning villages, leaving a smoking trail strewn with the bodies of the
nobles and gentry behind him. He called to his ranks the peasantry; his
motley army pressed on victoriously in the name of freedom to the very
walls of Moscow. At the gates of the capital, his forces were at length
held in check by the Imperial Government. The outlaw chief was out-
witted, some say through treachery, and executed in 1676 beneath the
Kremlin walls. Before the 1917 Revolution, Razin had become a folklore
hero; since that time he has been the central figure of numerous plays,
operas, and ballets. Vassili Kamenski has best recorded his exploits for the
new theatre in his energetic, poetic study of this meteoric character, which
initially reached the stage in première at the Moscow Art Theatre.

Hardly less important than the events surrounding the career of Stenka
Razin are those associated with the revolt of Emilian Pugachev, who,
during the reign of Catherine the Great, joined peasants and national
minorities in a menacing uprising which briefly shook the security of the
throne. The rebellion is particularly significant today because the small,
dissatisfied non-Russian groups here first voiced openly their murmuring
discontent against imperial jailers. The Union has found a way, where the
former government failed, to solve the perplexing problems of race minorities; and for this reason, in retrospect, the Pugachev Revolution glows
with added lustre. Trenev has translated these episodes to the stage in a
play which Markov, the Russian critic, calls "monumental drama." Trenev,
casting romance aside, realistically analyzes the circumstances which
produced the rebellion and interprets these causes with contemporary
significance. His play and other Pugachev dramatizations have had great
popularity with the Soviet audiences.

The Kamenski and Trenev dramas might be called ancient history. The
more recent events leading to the Revolution have also been celebrated
again and again in the Soviet Theatre. The revolt of the military upon
the accession of Nicholas I to the throne—foreshadowing the mutiny of
the army in the World War—has been dramatically portrayed in
Venksteri's *1825*. Shapovalenko has written two important chronicles, the
first of which, *1881*, describes with steel-like directness the assassination of
Tzar Alexander; the second, *Georg Gapon,* recalls the horrible massacre of
January 1905 when the guns of the royalist guardsmen swept down men,

women, and children who had gathered before the Winter Palace to beg the Little White Father for bread. The play takes its name from the priest who on that Bloody Sunday led the petitioning masses to the banks of the Neva. Loshkin's *The Ninth of January* commemorates the same sad and brutal massacre.

There are other plays of historical significance, which do not deal directly with the sequent events culminating in the February Days but which visualize political life in Russia under Tzarist rule. These are prone to spot the story of the past in the light of prejudice, very much as American studies of the War of Secession have inclined, until very recently, toward a Northern interpretation. Of such kind are Shegolov's *The Empress' Conspiracy,* Chedievsky's *Alexander I,* Shapovalenko's *Peter,* and Lerner's *Nicholas First.* The dramatic prototype for all dramas of this group could well be studied in *Tzar Feydor,* made famous long before the social upheaval by the Moscow Art Theatre. However striking these plays of prelude may be, they pale before the stage record of the Revolution proper. The February Days, the abdication, the two-faced Kerenski government, the spectacular revolt of Kornilov (melting in nothingness as it neared the gates of the Hermitage), and the October victory are sure-fire stories for the dramatists.

The gunsmoke had hardly cleared from the Leningrad streets before plays were recalling those moments of strong living and elemental emotion. The first dramas of Revolution spread themselves into mass pageants. For a time it seemed, indeed, that the people were bent on turning all plays into gigantic spectacles, to be enacted under the open sky by vast groups of players rivaling the audience in size. Surely there must have been an indescribable thrill in watching the *Liberation of Labor,* a symbolic representation of the overthrow of Church and State, ending with the triumph of the Red Forces; or in witnessing actors, six thousand strong, reconstruct the *Taking of the Winter Palace* on the original location with a climax including gun-fire from the battleship on the Neva. The overwrought, jumbled confusion of the plays was symbolic of the first burst of enthusiasm of the masses. Sincere and crude, they held the center stage for their hour of usefulness, and then were gone and forgotten except in the annals of that decade.

The mediæval church moved its propaganda drama from altar to city square; the revolt of the masses moved its propaganda drama from the market-place into the forsaken playhouses. Meyerhold was in command as Revolutionary theatre leader. He was ranking radical spirit, and his post came automatically to him. He produced *The Mystery Bouffe,* the poet

Maiakovski's emotionalization of the passing of the old order, and *Earth Prancing*. Cycle plays, which suggest marked technical likeness to the miracle and mystery plays of the Dark Ages, relayed whole sections of the Revolution to willing and waiting auditors. Sometimes these cycles traced at tedious length and with snail's pace the growth of the cause from 1671 to the fall of the Kerenski government. The wiser playwright was satisfied to confine himself to a smaller section of the panorama of history and stage its events more critically. Sukhanov's *1917* was one of the most elaborate of the cycle pieces and is less lurid and hysterical than most of the writings of this phase of the new theatre. Today the playwrights are beginning to survey this period with greater sanity and composure. Already a glimpse of a more rational approach may be seen in the libretto for *Quiet Flows the Don*, in *The Watchmaker and the Chicken*, or in Korneichuk's *The Truth*.

The Civil War dogged directly and relentlessly upon the heels of the Revolution. The scene of this greater struggle was the entire map of the new Republic. The Revolution had been fought out for the most part in the great industrial centers, especially Leningrad. The Civil War found its battlefield extending from Siberia to the Latvian border and southward to the Black Sea. The Revolution had neither the emotional nor the physical latitudes which the struggle to the death between the Red and the White forces offered to the playwrights. To enlarge the already sufficiently large canvas, the foreign powers entered the picture. Some believe that this interference in the Russian affairs aided the Red Cause tremendously in that it gave the Bolshevics a much needed sense of unity against the foreign invader, a situation not unlike that produced by Austria's entry into the French Revolution. At any rate, the Intervention provided the playwrights with tense moments and powerful situations which imagination clothed with nationalistic as well as doctrinaire fervor.

Furmanov's *Rebellion* transports the audience to the center of the Red Army in Asia. Vishnevsky writes an episodic account, mingling tears with laughter, petty details with mighty issues, of the Budenny Campaign, and calls it *The First Cavalry Army*. Kirschon fashions the death of the Commissars at Baku into a gripping play, *The City of High Winds*, which later becomes more famous as an opera libretto. Serafinovich in *The Iron Flood* (a dramatization of the novel) selects an incident wherein the Red Army is cut off from its base in the Caucasus. Threatened with annihilation, privation, and disease, the soldiers hold their own until relief comes. The realism of the text has been given an even more realistic production by the young disciple of Meyerhold, Okhlopkov. Bill-Belotserkovski's *Storm* and Fadeyev's *The Nineteen* are further pages from the diary of battles for the Soviet State.

Too often the diary technique supplants the mechanics of dramaturgy with the result that many of these plays are records only. They are, like Elizabethan chronicle plays, filled with multitudinous details of war and personalities, which register nothing upon an audience which has not absorbed a background sufficient to supply the missing links of the argument. Yet the dramas, like the older chronicle plays, are intentionally contemporary in appeal and do not, generally, attempt universality. For this reason many of them deserve nothing better than to be quietly and quickly forgotten.

Some few there are of these Civil War chronicles which legitimately may make a bid for a place in world-theatre repertory. Because of the care-ful production and liberal interpretation current in the Soviet Union, the shoddy qualities of a text may be disguised by the radiant materials of performance to such a degree, indeed, that glittering appears like true golden lustre. Of such nature is the confusing problem presented by Tairov's direction of Vishnevski's *Optimistic Tragedy*.

The theme is the acquisition of the Russian Fleet by the Bolshevic Com-missars in 1918. The flagship is held by a large and powerful group of the anarchists. The Soviet Commissar arrives from Moscow to take command. To the surprise of the soldiers and officers, the Commissar is a woman. At first the able-bodied seamen think that this is a joke, but gradually discover that she is not a comic opera coloratura. She is confronted by conspiracies and counter-conspiracies; but, of course, she wins. Death comes hand in hand with her moment of triumph, but she meets the last foe confidently because she knows the anarchist order is dead. She feels sure that the new government is marching on and inevitably will dissipate future opposition. The personal note is submerged beneath the mass ideal. A single death for the Cause becomes optimistic tragedy.

One scene in particular exhibits sturdy melodramatic power, especially when Alice Kuhnen plays the Commissar. The sailors led by a stoker refuse to submit to the authority of the woman envoy from the Kremlin. They will not give in to petticoat rule. They try to intimidate her and, failing that, start to use physical violence. "Are you joking?" she cries. They tell her with proper seamen's emphasis that they never joke. She draws a pistol and shoots the stoker. "Nor do I," she retorts. In her reply the whole spirit of the Bolshevic Revolution seems to speak.

The *Optimistic Tragedy* is only one of several naval plays. Vishnevski has also written *We from Kronstadt*. The belief in the superiority of

The Optimistic Tragedy increases tenfold when it is compared with Korneichuk's *The Last of the Squadron*, which, although it received a prize in the Ukranian State Theatre, is a piddling sort of job, disjointed in the writing, filled with long arid stretches mercifully enlivened by native vaudeville and a spectacular and deafening final curtain. There is such a thing as sound and fury signifying nothing.

Of finer grain than these water melodramas is Ivanov's *The Armored Train*, recorded in quick, staccato scenes which hold the attention and touch the heart. The Siberian peasants, lacking adequate arms and leaders, are bartering their bodies against the powder of the White Army under Kolchak. The brief rapid episodes of the play describe in theatrical short-hand how these untrained and unequipped loyalists effect the capture of an armored car. Two moments especially are true theatre. The physical and mental collapse of the White officer, trapped in the control-cab, may be compared favorably with the cell scene in Galsworthy's *Justice*. And stronger yet, the terror which fills the spectator when the Chinese peasant throws himself on the rails to stop the oncoming armored train is realism plus. Ivanov writes hard, impersonal, surly drama, without needless embellishments or decorations. The Gorki Art production of this play is as stark and as icy as the text itself. This is not drama for escapists.

A much more human play than *The Armored Train* is *Lyubov Yarovaya*, written by K. A. Trenev, one of the earliest of Soviet playwrights. Against a background of civil war, cluttered with episodes of marching men, storming of prisons, mining of bridges, evacuations and re-evacuations of cities first by the Whites and then by the Reds, this playwright sympathetically reveals the personal struggle of a woman, Lyubov, a little schoolmistress whose husband is a White spy in the Red Army. She is also politically minded, but an ardent Revolutionist. The old conflict of love struggles for supremacy with duty. Lyubov Yarovaya is not for all that a melodramatic character as Trenev pleases to present her; she is facing a profound dilemma which touches the borderland of honest tragedy.

Besides the domestic, human interest, the play outlines minutely the material difficulties which hampered the Communist Party during the Civil War. The lack of resources, the untrained troops, the uncertainty of peasant support, and above all the treachery of individuals hysterically attempting to pick the winning side fill the scenes. It was a day of opportunists. To combat these inefficiencies and uncertain supporters, it was necessary for Party members to assume tasks for which they were totally unfitted but which they did willingly, although not always adequately.

The objective understanding with which Trenev handles these diversified elements of plot, atmosphere, and character, and blends them into an acceptable dramatic unit discloses a sense of perspective greater than might have been expected in a play written within the hours of high nervous tension. His latest historical drama, *The Banks of the Neva,* confirms the promise of his earlier work.

The Fighters by Romashov studies the Civil War from within the ranks of the Soviet Army. The protagonists here are not Whites and Reds, nor is the conflict between love and duty. The problem is more intimate and is centered in the pathetic story of the old-school army officer trying to adjust himself to the disciples and methods of the new régime. Lenchitski has been well trained in military affairs, his knowledge is of great value to the Soviet, but he fails to understand a democratic army code. For him the old German system is the logical and only way. He cannot comprehend why his own youthful student-soldiers can be more closely attuned to this proletarian philosophy than he. He resents the implication that he is a conservative, for he has grown old in devoted service to the Revolution. At length he becomes altogether discouraged and confused by the whole business, and reluctantly decides to kill himself. His purpose is melodramatically interrupted by his Comrade, Olga. She seems to sense the situation, and begs him to carry on. He promises her not to give up but to learn as a beginner the new mass methods of discipline and efficiency.

The Fighters does not rely upon violent action or theatricalization for its driving power, which rises from the analysis of a single character. The figure of Lenchitski is presented so humanly that the strong dose of argument in behalf of mass control in military affairs is softened agreeably. For foreigners who have little interest in army problems under any régime, the play is likely to seem much ado about nothing. Its persistent popularity is, however, merited because of the distinguished performance which it is given at the State Maly Theatre. It is also on the regular repertories of the Theatre of the Red Army and the Ermolova Studio, and is played frequently in all the dramatic centers. For the Union it presents a thesis of emotional adjustment which many have experienced bitterly.

Another phase of Civil War wholly different from that portrayed in *Yarovaya,* *The Armored Train,* and *The Fighters* was provided by the interference of the Allied Forces in Soviet affairs. This military occupation in defense of foreign interests brought to the theatre many plays. Prut's *1919* unfolds the heroic struggle against an atmospheric setting of Baku. Slavin utilizes the story of the French occupation of Odessa and writes *Intervention,* an arresting melodrama of conspiracy, treachery, and murder. The eloquent suspense provided by the singing laundresses who, through the intonation of their song, warn the conspirators of the approach of friend and foe, and the prolonged suspense of the arrest at the water-front café are incidental to the central thought: the enemy is helpless before the tactics of passive resistance and organized propaganda.

The Bolshevic forces know only too well the impossibility of defeating the occupationists in open battle. The French hold the seaport with seasoned troops, well equipped with food and ammunition. Yet slowly the secret agents of the Reds undermine the morale of the enemy soldiers. The desire to return home becomes so strong in the poilus' hearts that they mutiny, kill their officers, and demand an immediate return to France. The last scene of the play convincingly represents the embarking of the French legionnaires. Along with them go the frightened, defeated bour-geois merchants of Odessa who have profited under the intervention and who, in the eyes of the Soviet audiences, have sold their country for ill-earned gains. Their lot is exile.

Intervention has attracted international attention, chiefly for the strik-ing production given the play at the Vakhtangov Theatre. The settings, designed by Rabinovich, are extremely effective. The waterfront café, the office of the French Commander, and particularly the Great Steps of Odessa, which in final tableau the Red Soldiers climb with their French comrade,—all these merit the applause of foreign enthusiasts. Rabino-vich, in true Vakhtangov fashion, has mingled the real and the unreal most successfully. He has cleverly emphasized the naturalistic elements without photographic reproduction. Doubtless the stimulating memories that *Intervention* has left upon thousands of spectators are fully as much a tribute to his stagecraft as to Slavin's playwriting. Designer and author share in this eloquent testament against war.

The Optimistic Tragedy, Intervention, Yarovaya, and *The Armored Train* are representatives of the better plays born of the Revolution. Each has discernible qualities of excellence which recommend it to the theatre enthusiast. The type of theatre which they represent has inherent faults. It is difficult to adapt the episodes of the news-reel to the stage. Historical plays have always faced this problem. From Shakspere's *Henry VI* down to Drinkwater's *Abraham Lincoln* and *Cromwell,* a series of dramatic productions have failed to rise above the episodes which they compass. These Soviet plays share the usual shortcomings. Yet they are often fervent, honest, and overardent in driving home the issue, frequently using the

triphammer to make assurance doubly sure. Subtlety is not their long
suit. Recent contributions like Pogodin's *The Man with a Rifle*, Yan-
ousky's *A Ballad of Britanka* and Nikitin's *Apsheron Night* fail to show
marked improvement over those historical dramas written a decade ago.
Two playwrights *have* triumphed over the customary obstacles of the
chronicle type, and have succeeded in writing plays which are timely and
gentle in preaching. One has been a world figure in the theatre for many
years and a father to revolt—Maxim Gorki. The other is a son of the
Revolution; his name is Michael Bulgakov.

Bulgakov was born in Kiev in 1891. He was a doctor. He is now an
actor, producer, novelist, and dramatist. He has been intimately associated in various capacities with the Moscow Art Theatre. His life has
been dotted by innumerable difficulties with the governmental authorities
and censors whom he once was bold enough to satirize in his play *Purple
Island*. At heart it is likely he is an individualist. He struggles valiantly
to appear collective minded. His *Molière* found itself on the black list
because it stressed the private life of the dramatist and not his social
contribution. So did his *Last of the Turbins* when it was first presented.
The conservative element in the Party felt this play represented the
counter-Revolutionists too sympathetically. Bulgakov failed to burlesque
his White Army officers or turn them into villains. Was this heresy?
Reason eventually won. *The Last of the Turbins*, once presented, became
a permanent and extremely popular part of the repertory of the Gorki
Art Theatre. From the angle of art censorship, the play is significant in
that its production marked a curbing of the left wing Revolutionists in
the new theatre, and gave precedent for a broader discussion of life on the
Soviet stage.

The Last of the Turbins, though now ten years old, is still one of the
best plays inspired by the Revolution and the Civil War. The Turbin
family are residents of Kiev during those uncertain hours when White
and Red Armies struggled for supremacy in the Ukraine. The brothers
of the household are officers in the White Army. The sister is married to
a German official. Scene by scene, with quiet tragic force, the fortunes of
the middle-class Turbins and the cause which they represent crumble. The
Hetman abdicates in cowardly fashion and his rule of the Ukraine falls;
the gorilla warrior Petliura engulfs the Kiev district in a sadistic sea of
brutality. The fine-feathered German allies desert. The elder brother
is killed; the younger is cruelly wounded. Above the household hover the
birds of ill omen. The last act takes place on Christmas Eve. The broken

and impoverished Turbins pathetically struggle to observe the festival with the customary elaborateness of better days. As the final curtain descends, the Bolshevic troops, singing the *Internationale,* enter the much disputed city. The family listening at the open window realize that the old times are gone forever. They sense that they must begin again, that they must build new lives in a new world; but they are not afraid.

Character dominates plot. There are melodramatic scenes to be sure. Fixed in the memory are the unforgetable moments of the fight in the schoolhouse, or the grueling animation of Bolbuton, Petliura's lieutenant, who burns out the eyes of a Jewish peasant with a kerosene lamp on a trumped-up charge of espionage. Such grim theatrical scenes as these are bound to leave a lasting imprint upon the mind, but the private tragedy accompanying the failure of bourgeois economic systems still remains the center of emotional appeal. In this respect, the play has true universality. Solid in technique and strong in situation, the drama of the Turbins stands a modern masterpiece. There are many Turbin families in the Soviet Union. That their lot is difficult the new order recognizes. Bulgakov has done his best to make the passing of a social class dramatically immortal.

Bulgakov started his career after the October Days. Maxim Gorki has been recognized as a world dramatist since *The Lower Depths* first appeared in 1902. A year before his death he was publicly honored with the Order of Lenin "for his literary services to the working class and toilers in the U. S. S. R." and acknowledged as first Soviet dramatist and writer. Gorki was ever a realist. He did not need the Revolution to teach him that philosophy of art. That he possessed unusual creative power both in the novel and in the theatre, no one can deny. He probably never thought of himself particularly as a dramatist. He was, like George Bernard Shaw, a philosopher, who found in the drama a convenient tool for presenting his thoughts to the public. In this respect he anticipated the creed of a utilitarian theatre. *The Enemies, Mother,* and *Merchants* (dramatizations of novels) give some weight to this idea. That he felt the crises of the social order keenly and could reveal them in graphic character studies is a cardinal strength of his literary genius. That he could be at the same time a belligerent reformer without haranguing like a soap-box orator is certainly to his credit.

His drama on the prelude to revolution, *Egor Bulychev,* is no exception to the talents elsewhere exhibited. Action, as usual, is subordinated to the people of his story. The unity of the piece is realized through the characterization rather than through skillful playmaking. He was in no sense a follower of Sardou or Ibsen. *Egor* was intended as the first part of a trilogy on the Revolution. The second part, *Dostigayev and Others,* was finished before Gorki died. The third part never found expression. The purpose which Gorki had in mind was to demonstrate through this trilogy that the Revolution was the inevitable finish of a society founded upon the ownership of private property. He is not anxious, therefore, to present the historical events upon the scene. He does present, rather, an analysis of the background for these momentous events as typified in a series of exciting personalities.

Bulychev is a wealthy merchant, but he has not always been a merchant. He came from the people, married into the bourgeoisie, and has lent his brains to increase the worldly goods of his adopted class. Death is near. His body is filled with cancer. Raven relatives croak about him, impatient for the time to come when his property will legally pass on to them. Bulychev sees a parallel between his physical condition and his avaricious kin. He believes further that the decay of his body and the decay of an outworn social régime have much in common. He will not last much longer; neither will this middle-class society. Money and cancer amount to the same thing—destruction. Barrie once used a similar parallelism in *The Will,* but Gorki has planted the theme more deeply in the social order. Dramatically he has accomplished a very difficult task. He has retained sympathy for Egor as a personality, but created a hatred against that for which he stands.

In *Egor Bulychev* the character of Dostigayev appears. In the second part of the trilogy this Western European-American merchant becomes the center of interest on Gorki's stage. *Dostigayev and Others* is a play of the forty days in which the Kerenski régime comes under the scrutiny of the dramatist. Again he lashes a social order bent on accumulating personal wealth and ignoring the tidal wave which is soon to sweep all this hoarded treasure away forever. The play was first presented in 1933. It has never won the popularity of the first part of the unfinished trilogy.

It is a long jump from this psychological analysis of revolutionary causes to the temperamental, spontaneous *Taking of the Winter Palace* with its six thousand actors. Art refines reality; reflection and philosophy temper the violence of elemental physical action. Themes of revolution can produce great plays or bad dramatic potboilers. The results are commensurate with the power of the playwrights. It is not unfair, surely, to remark that *The Last of the Turbins* and *Egor Bulychev* both came from the pens of men with literary training of pre-Revolutionary days.

Enthusiasm in the theatre is excellent; enthusiasm plus tried experience writes better plays. Many of the faults of the playwrights of revolution are doubtless the faults of inexperience. Will they learn? Some fail through too much zeal; some, because of slight ability. Appreciation of an art is not necessarily accompanied by creative power. Belief in Communism is not necessarily the first essential for writing a good play. Some few have demonstrated that they are artists; others are learning. The plays born of revolution have been an excellent training school, at least, for the Soviet playwright of tomorrow.

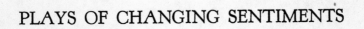

PLAYS OF CHANGING SENTIMENTS

VII

Plays of Changing Sentiments

IN TWO DECADES of existence the Soviet Union has progressed so far and so rapidly in industry, in agriculture, in sanitation, and in developing boundless natural resources that its achievements with the aid of a little imagination assume the outline of miracles. To the Comrades, the doubled triumph of the Five Year Plan is a perpetual source of self-satisfaction, which is often not accompanied by modesty. The thoughtful stranger suspects that the results have exceeded the most optimistic expectations of the people and that their breathless pride is mingled with frank surprise. It has all been an exciting game, played, for the most part, in true sporting spirit. The race toward centralized industrialization has strengthened immeasurably the sinews of the State and the dictatorship of the Proletariat.

Never lagging behind the economic and political advances, the changes in domestic relationships have accelerated the growth of a new system of education and social ethics which exhibit gains equal to those of farms and factories. The phenomenal increase of a reading public, avid for learning, parallels the mushroom records in steel and brick. This intellectual renaissance is all very spectacular but not inexplicable. The human being develops more rapidly between the years of one and twenty than between the years of twenty and forty. The Union has had its first twenty years. The terrific tempo will undoubtedly slow down in the middle-age of this new Republic.

The theatre has reflected the Five Year Plans and the new program of social relationships. It has been a conscientious and valuable ally of the government in explaining each new theory, in stimulating the tardy, hesitant, lethargic masses to action, and in fostering the thrill of achievement in the people. All plays are in a broader sense dramas of social relationships. When the new theatre holds the mirror up to life, it is not so progressive after all. The deviation which the Soviet stage makes from the usual rôle is that the social problem of the mass is stressed rather than that of the individual. The personal element is subordinated to the Cause. This approach to theatre produces a great library of plays that seem strange, oftentimes unconvincing, to the Western World, which does not understand, or is reluctant to tolerate if it does understand, the underlying philosophy.

To the Soviet audience the tragic content of *The Second Mrs. Tanqueray* would likely appear comic or futile, because the thesis involves a sex relationship which the Union would sense as a stupid bourgeois convention. "Such foolishness," it would say, "couldn't happen here. All of Paula's difficulties could have been avoided by injecting a little calm realism into the false sentimentality of the situation." Plays in which young men sweat blood to conquer Wall Street might appear to the Soviet audience selfish and even immoral. Plays of sex or business based on rugged individualism become real to the Marxian audience only when they are presented in a satiric vein, or viewed as reports on the shortcomings of a capitalistic society. *Saint Joan,* for example, at the Kamerny is played as a satire on religion. Such a performance is natural and honest in Moscow and has no intention of rivaling a Black Mass.

On the other hand New York saw *Red Rust,* and many found the play vulgar. "It proves that the U. S. S. R. won't last long," said some, who by that remark indicated clearly an inability to recognize that from a Soviet point of view the piece is a critical invective against the early abuses of the new social ethics and not a naturalistic photograph of crowded living conditions in the student quarter. Broadway is ironically amused by the young Communist who makes love in the language of bolts and steel rivets. The Sverdlova is amused by the young American who makes love in a jargon about cars, cocktail parties, and the amassing of private fortunes. On Broadway the sympathy in Kirschon's *Bread* would very likely be with the Kulak, because America, in general, does not accept the premises upon which collective farming is based and would look upon anyone who opposed these as a hero. How impossible it is to judge these Soviet plays of social adjustment and achievement by the standards accepted on this side of the Atlantic! Since the new theatre stresses the premise that art is not apolitical, these Soviet plays can never be truly appreciated apart from the issues which they represent.

What importance does the collective farm and the reconstruction of the village hold for the playwrights in the new theatre? In 1929 and 1930, after famine had killed unbelievable numbers, the Government decided to insure the nation against food shortage and, further, to develop a foreign market for surplus grain. The principal obstacle was the farmer, particularly the wealthy farmer. The country villages were hopelessly backward; the output of the soil was far below normal. Against a determined opposition, the principles of social economy dictated the program—the farm

collective. Force was resorted to at first, but was later tempered by persua-
sion. The collective won (or as was said, "the tractor won"), with some
concessions on the Government side and not without bloodshed and bitter-
ness. The reluctant individual was crushed beneath the mass ideal. A new
sanitary village took the place of the old and a new agriculture popularized
the tractor in place of the ancient wooden plow. This is the un-American
background against which the Soviet playwright constructs his agrarian
drama.

Though this is material foreign to America, it is, nevertheless, good
material for the theatre, and the Soviet theatre makes the most of it. Plays
about the stupid peasant and the ghastly immoral life of the village are as
old as Russia itself. Tolstoi's *The Power of Darkness* is a horrible picture
of the degenerate and hopeless existence in the days before the War. But
the new plays are not content to observe; they are concerned with changing
the lives of men. Sordidness is subordinated to quiet confidence in the new
order, and, like the war plays, with ultimate victory for the Cause.
Seilfulina's novel *Virinea,* which was later adapted to the stage, introduces
the village peasant fighting against education and fiercely planting his foot
against progress. The very popular drama, *The End of Krivorlish* by
Romashev, continues the same theme. Yanovsky's *Fury* is in the same key.
The revised version of *Resurrection* studies the peasant in a new critical
light.

The collective farm proper rather than the rehabilitation of the village
is the main issue in Stavski's *At a Run,* staged so radically and successfully
in Moscow by Okhlopkov. Better than this is Leonov's *The Badgers,* again
a dramatization of a novel, in which the peasantry fights against the
requisitions made by the Party for grain. The landholders are overcome
because they are without organization or single purpose. Again and again
the idea is emphasized that victory resulted because mass thought was
pitted against individualistic selfishness. Trenev caught something of
Defoe's key in *In a Bright Meadow,* where horses realize the value of the
soil collective better than the Yahoo peasants. Virta's *Land* discusses the
problem of counter-revolutionists in the Tambor Province. As adequate
as any of the plays of remaking the peasant, liquidating the Kulak, and
educating the agricultural community to the new ideology is Kirschon's
Bread.

Kirschon, though he cannot satisfy the Party, is one of the most
promising dramatists of the U. S. S. R. He has been prominent in the
organization of Soviet writers. He has repeatedly proved his power as a
dramatist. Among his plays are *Red Rust,* written with Uspensky and

played in New York, *The Rails Hum,* and *The City of Winds.* He was awarded the prize in the national play contest for *The Miraculous Alloy.* *The Great Day* has been accepted by the Vakhtangov Theatre and is pending production. When he started to write *Bread,* he did not come by his material second handed. He was an actual worker for the Party in the struggle with the Kulak. He knew through personal observation the districts which he describes in thrilling scenes.

Bread is more than an editorial story about the grain requisitions. Kirschon explains, with an open eye to good theatre, the village, the Kulak, and the peasant. To the economic problem he adds an important domestic touch in the character of Olga, the wife of the Commissar Mikhailov, who deserts her husband, when agrarian affairs are darkest, to consort with Pavel, a friend of the Commissar's and a Comrade. The glamor of a man recently returned from Berlin fires Olga's vanity and feminine sense of conquest. The Cause becomes a vague philosophy in proportion to her personal desires. It is perhaps needless to say that the picture is not presented sympathetically.

Above the vivid and exciting scenes of battle, domestic and civil, the detailed characterization of Mikhailov rises in importance and serves not only as the keystone of dramatic interest, but also exemplifies the spirit of the good Party member—kindly, reasonable, but always determined. He will permit neither personal danger nor private suffering to interfere with his service to the State. He subjects himself wholly to the mass will. He has a job to do. That job in this particluar play is to collect grain, and nothing must stop him. There is no doubt that *Bread* is a propaganda piece, but it is equally sure that Kirschon, in forging art into a weapon for the Cause, does not neglect his responsibilities to the theatre as a dramatist. *Bread* is a significant contribution to the plays of the agrarian front.

The triangle complication in *Bread* presents another issue in which the new theatre may well be interested. When Olga decides to leave Mikhailov and turns to Pavel, the old, old theatrical "two equals three" crops up for the solution which the theatre never solves. The outcome, as Kirschon sees it, is far removed from the doctrine of "till death do us part." Mikhailov raises not a finger to hold his wife. Since he is the ideal Communist, he must solve domestic relationships in the ideal way. Olga must do what she thinks is best. He must not try to hold her against her will. The independence and real equality of the Soviet woman has necessarily created a new type of hero and heroine for the theatre. The drama of possession has passed into nothingness as far as the *Theatre at the Left* is concerned. When the middle-class lady with middle-class morals enters the scene, she is ridiculed. When she leaves the stage weeping, she is not the subject for pity, but for contempt. The Western European heroine has played her last part as leading lady on the Soviet stage; she is now the comedienne. The new theatre is crowded with energetic eight-cylinder Noras, who give little time to the misunderstood middle-class Torvalds. Bulgakov's *Zoika's Flat*, produced at the Vakhtangov, is a good example of this advanced type of domestic drama. Anatole Glebov's *Inga* analyzes the Soviet woman and extols the new heroine.

Inga represents the human machine which must be admired because it contributes so much to a progressive, utilitarian society, but which, even for the devotees of new womanhood, lacks something in desirable feminine qualities. Inga is the superworker: Mera is the superintellectual, who has become so absorbed in the Cause that she has lost all sense of proportion. Glafeera, in contrast to the other two, is really the new leading lady and represents the type which the new social philosophy most admires. She is the new woman at her best. Although humiliated by her husband's desertion, she courageously faces life as it is, and starts out to recreate a place for herself in a world which she can claim as her very own. She learns to be a first-class worker, self-reliant in every way. But she still retains her feminine charm, and her delight in her children never falters. She is subject to no man; she has found the supreme joy of belonging to herself. She is truly free. Rumor says that the Union is a woman's world. Plays like Glebov's *Inga* indicate that it is not a man's world. The theatre teaches that it is a world of honest equality and of an active, not philosophical, single standard.

So radical a readjustment of sex relationships was upsetting in the beginning even to the Union. To the dismay of many a Communist, the new woman offered an opportunity for personal exploitation and social confusion greater than had the woman of the old era. The abuses of this earlier period were an open target for well-directed criticism in *Constantine Terekhin* (Kirschon's *Red Rust*). Terekhin is an ardent advocate of equality for women and the single standard, but he is at heart a hypocrite. He employs the new social privileges as a mask to disguise and justify his own promiscuity. Through the high office which he holds he takes unfair advantage of all who come near him. He abuses the marriage rights. When the suicide of one young woman too obviously names him as the cause, he is denounced by the "cell" and dismissed from the Party. The domestic front provides good theatre material for the Soviet dramatist.

The Union does not always look at life with a long face. Misunderstand-ings of this fact are current in Western Europe and America. The com-munist can laugh as well as the capitalist. One of the most amusing plays on the marriage question is Katayev's comedy *Squaring the Circle*. In this round of obvious farce cut to a balanced Sardou pattern, the bourgeois domesticity is soundly satirized in the character of a young bride, Ludmilla. Her running-mate, Tonya, the superintellectual bride, is also represented with tongue in cheek. These girls have married two young Communists and have set up housekeeping in a crowded room. It soon becomes evident that the marriage knot has been tied backwards. A divorce and another marriage shuffles the four people into a more satisfactory family arrange-ment. The light surface of fun thinly veils the trenchant satire against those who enter into hasty marriages. The play ridicules those who are so intellectual that they become dull to material necessities and those who are so bourgeois that the domestic interests stultify intellectual development. Comrade Flavius, a Soviet poet, throughout the play gives a humorous balance to the superficially plotted scenes.

Romance is again retailored in a novel and gay fashion in Finn's *Nonsense*. Anna meets an old admirer, who, because of the unrequited love which he held for her years ago, has lost his grip on life. She is very much moved by his pathetic display of devotion, but she is a realist. The solution is not, as she sees it, to mother or to marry the man. After some hesitation, she arrives at the decision that any male so overwhelmed by chronic lovesickness must be mentally unbalanced. The answer is not wedding-bells and soft music, but medical examination and treatment. The new heroine has, indeed, developed in this case a sharp sense of humor. She has no room in her philosophy for Bunthorne. Romeo, contemplating suicide in Friar Lawrence's cell, is not romantic; he is unhealthily abnormal.

Young love and mature love furnish the themes for farce and satire in the new theatre, and domestic relationships which do not portray the new man and the new woman also provide laughter for the audiences of the metropolitan centers. Selvinsky's *Umka the White Bear,* a delightful bit of foolishness set in an Eskimo igloo, portrays with robust humor the Arctic custom of sharing and exchanging wives. This northern broadmind-edness proves a little embarrassing to the devoted Communist, who is sacrificing comfort and health to bring the culture of Lenin to the tribes of the frozen wastes. Umka's untutored ignorance might be compared with the naïveté of Galatea in Gilbert's *Pygmalion*. It is very hard for Umka to catch the new ideology. His sense of social responsibility becomes muddled by the code of civilization.. The Arctic savage flounders badly when he tries to guide his conduct by the rule of the hammer and sickle. "There is nothing either good or bad but thinking makes it so." The Union does not always see eye to eye with New York; the tribal people do not always see eye to eye with the Soviet; Galatea did not see eye to eye with Pygmalion.

Though one may smile and break into a loud laugh over the reconstruction of the Arctic White Bear, there is not much humor in training a man schooled in prerevolutionary sophistication and learning to stand with clenched fist before the red flag. It is a hard and sometimes heartrending job to teach an old dog new tricks. Marxian relationships—easily accepted by the generation which has matured since the October Days—are insurmountable stumblingblocks to the middleaged. Inga, Anna, and Mikhailov represent those who, because they still had youth, could learn to place realism before emotion. These characters faced the problem of rationalization in marriage. Other emotional relationships likewise must be readjusted to the ideology. Friendship and loyalty must also be stripped of sentimentality and subordinated to mass interests.

The reëvaluation of sentiments is ready material for the new theatre. In Schtock's *The Car and Marion,* Vasya and Trakhamanenko, friends of long standing, find that years of association must be forgotten when the welfare of the State is in question. "Personal feelings cannot be allowed to betray the Proletariat's interests" has become a commandment of social conduct. The ironic tragedy of those too old to learn is clearly but none too sympathetically presented in Olesh's *A Conspiracy of Feelings,* where Ivan laments that "the once great emotions of life are now looked upon as unimportant and middle class."

Of the group who had become set in conventional schemes of conduct before 1917, the intellectual was the most deeply entrenched. The scholar has always pursued his undisputed way along the paths of thought; the artist was never forced to make his creations conform to utilitarian ends. Both had always considered themselves separated from life by privilege, because art, science, and literature had been in Russia, as they are now in America, apolitical. When the *beaux arts* and the sciences change color and lose their independence and are made servants of politics, social science, and economics—here is a change indeed.

The scientist dealing with divorced matter or with pure mathematics is confronted with no great problem, but the scientist concerned with the application of his research to practical affairs of daily life can easily deviate to the right or to the left in his conclusions. The confident song of academic freedom subsides into a wail now and again in the United States. It was not long ago that Tennessee objected to biology. The old order of Soviet intellectuals found that the new ideology denied it choice. Apolitical learning was a thing of the past. Failure to realize this meant there was no room for them under the dictatorship of the Proletariat.

Such was the problem which confronted the loyal Lenchitski in *The Fighters*. A new mass method of running armies was entirely contrary to the theory in which this military expert had been trained. He rebelled. There was only one way by which he could hold his place and that was to bow to the will of the people. It is never easy for those who have been leaders and tasted power to step aside and with good grace and a smile let their successors take over the controls. It is even harder for those who have never thought of themselves as a part of a political system to find themselves hubs of a political controversy. Such humiliation is akin to intellectual death, for many of the elders are no longer capable of learning a new way.

The Union has tried to be very charitable with those in whom the bourgeois philosophy was inculcated and have tried to find a place for them in the new scheme of things. The success has been only moderate. Stanislavsky saw the light with great difficulty; Meyerhold carried the torch, but failed to keep it burning. Those associated with university life have been particularly hard pressed. Many have found the new régime impossible and have concluded that death was easier than life. Afinogenov catches the emotions of the passing order very well, and attempts to explain the discarded intellectual to the public in his play entitled *Fear*.

Fear is the story of a college professor who was confirmed in the belief that his way was right. He was convinced that his work was his own personal possession, and that the results which came from his laboratories might be utilized as he wished. To discover that the Government respected his learning but had no intention of letting him do with it as he chose was indeed a bitter realization. To discover that his own laboratory assistants had been created his superiors drove him to despair and almost to madness. However, Afinogenov does not leave his pathetic character in his tragic dilemma. He suggests a means by which he can fight his way back to useful and respected service in this worker's state. The note upon which the play ends is highly optimistic in the Soviet Union; elsewhere it might be considered tragic.

Fear is an interesting but badly constructed play. The plot wanders and weaves about and includes extraneous material, which certainly does not heighten the theatrical effectiveness. If Afinogenov teaches Professor

Borodin a lesson in mass thinking, with a sop at the end, he has not found, necessarily, the answer for all intellectuals in the Union. Characters who are tinged with the stain of the non-conformist are represented without sympathy or as stupid and treacherous people. Although this attitude does not mar the stage effectiveness of the play, it does not build faith in the profundity of the analysis. The Soviet god in the machine can cut the Gordian knot at the close of a drama with a sickle. Afinogenov makes Marx descend on wires and feels that he has settled everything.

In *The Noose,* Afinogenov shifts ground from the older to the younger intellectual. Here the problem is that of the Bolshevic student who is in constant danger of wandering from the straight and narrow path into a "right or left deviation." This is a situation in which the youthful intellectual frequently finds himself, and one which is of considerable concern to the Powers. Faiko twice wrestled with this same thought. *Teacher Bubus* satirizes the intellectual talker and non-doer, for which particular type the Union has no use. He is a non-producer, and in a land of workers there is no need for him. *Egrav Seeks Adventure* discusses the ease with which the æsthete may become swayed by false philosophies and drawn into situations which place him in disfavor with the ideologies of the U. S. S. R. Egrav does not master his problems. Bad companions teach him questionable truths. He comes to a bad end. *The Man With a Portfolio* is written in the same key.

The intelligentsia has ever been a problem when government has attempted to regulate philosophy and artistic creation. Old Russia had to contend with Tolstoi and Gorki and Lunarcharski and certainly with Lenin. The new government is facing a like issue which cannot be settled this time by calling in the tractors or increasing the output of a ball-bearing factory. The question cannot be concluded by a Kremlin vote. Meanwhile the theatre probably will continue to present plays about the death of the old intellectuals and the deviations of the new.

If there is some uncertainty about the ultimate fate of the intellectuals, there is certainty and to spare about the success of the two Five Year Plans. The factories have invaded the theatres. Plays of industrialization are filled with exuberant spirit and confidence which sweep audiences off their feet in a wave of enthusiasm for "our" State. Bill-Belotserkovski contributed two dramas, dating back to the ancient history of the N. E. P. *Calm* and *Lull* in chronological position become plays of prelude to a later period of greater activity. Gladkov's *Cement,* a dramatization, records the socialization of industry, but pays some attention to the changing domestic affairs. Katayev's *Time Forward* and Kirschon's *The Rails Hum* suggest in their

titles the onrush of the building program and the frenzied haste to mech-
anize a nation.

The romance of nuts, bolts, tractors, dams, riveting machines, and
steam shovels stimulates little creative urge in the normal American playwright. That so many plays have been wrought out of these things of
wood and stone and steel proves that the inanimate has intrigued a multitude of Soviet writers. Their inspirations, however, have too frequently
resulted in dramas of mechanism much less lifelike than the machines
about which they were written.

Worthy of attention among the romancers of fly-wheels and plaster is
Nikolai Pogodin. He is in his late thirties. He was born of peasant stock
and had no opportunity for schooling other than that which he picked up
by himself along the route and through his association with the press, principally *Pravda*. In the veriest sense, he is a playwright of the Proletariat.
That he has been able to create moderately good plays out of almost
impossible material speaks in his praise.

All his dramas are the outgrowth of intimate contact with industrialization. Pride and fervor fill every scene. *The Poem of the Axe* sings the
song of accomplishment in the field of metallurgic discovery. A new steel
alloy can be a mighty force for increasing production. *Tempo* throbs with
the struggle in a construction unit against sabotage, misunderstanding, and
disease. The ignorance of the peasant worker, for the first time trying his
hand as mason and carpenter, is appalling. Typhoid stalks through the
camp. The peasants believe that the medical corps is poisoning the water.
A mutiny flares up and is fanned by saboteurs to dangerous proportions.
Disease is bad enough, but lack of health eduction is worse. The progress
of work is interrupted, and the lives of hundreds of sullen workmen, who
refuse to permit the infected to be taken to the hospitals or isolated, are
imperiled. Here is a tough knot for a young engineer like Boldyrev to
untie. He refuses to be beaten by the odds. The work in spite of hardships
and disloyalty is carried through in better than record time. A new tempo
has been established. Weak as this play is in technique, it is strong in
purpose, enthusiasm, and knowledge of its characters.

The Aristocrats, a later drama built on the same plan, is a much more
finished piece. The Baltic-White Sea Canal is in the building. The workers
are not peasants this time. They are the prostitutes, the thieves, the scum
of the great cities who have been detailed to this work as a form of penal
servitude. The spirit of the entire group is thoroughly nihilistic, but their
wits are sharper than those of the ignorant farmers. Again the work is
forced to pause while the leaders convert the prisoners to a fresh outlook

upon life. The story pictures an impressive but stark slice of life in which this riffraff from the metropolitan centers is born anew, and is slowly and patiently reclaimed through hard work for a life of respected citizenship. The tempo here is a double one: the physical construction of the canal and the mental and spiritual reconstruction of human beings. The audience shares with the actors the emotional thrill of watching the first ship pass through the completed waterway. "We have done it. It is our canal." The Red Army officers might well add their voices to the cheers of the workers: "We have remade men."

The Aristocrats has been given an excellent semi-realistic production at the Vakhtangov, which has blended acting and scenery and text into an impressive unity. Okhlopkov rivals this splendid production at the Krassnaya-Pressnya. The scenery and the costumes are here of slight importance. The inward spirit of the play, exquisitely revealed in rhythmic measures, receives the emphasis rather than the story. These two productions of Pogodin's *Aristocrats* form a startling contrast in the acting theory and stagecraft of the new theatre. Each is perfect within its peculiar scope.

Pogodin's *My Friend* again extols the new man that socialism has created. As Kirschon idealized the hero of the agrarian front in *Bread*, so Pogodin idealizes the hero of the industrial front in his play. The action, as usual in the "tempo dramas," takes place in the midst of the busy confusion of factory construction. The stock difficulties arise over and over only to be surmounted in the customary fashion. In an endless chain the workers march on to the next job and the next. The play stresses the thought that the work of creating a Socialist State never ends and that building a classless society is the most desirable occupation any man can have. With optimism and confidence which are almost disconcerting, these dramas of shafts and scaffolding, cement and railroad-ties, sing clarion clear of the triumph of manual labor.

Pogodin might be styled a natural writer of plays. He is not a sure technician. He loves life and has great confidence in it. He understands the working people and believes that a classless world may be achieved. The years show that as he taught himself in youth, he is continuing to teach himself in the art of the theatre. He is growing in dramatic power. Markov calls the hero of *My Friend*, SOCIALISM'S OWN MAN. It would not be wrong to call Pogodin, SOCIALISM'S OWN PLAYWRIGHT. For all his shortcomings, this son of the masses has found drama in industrialization and colloquial eloquence in the mechanical processes of building.

The drama of social relationships has never limited its interests to the U. S. S. R. "The Soviet knows no borders" is a slogan that has frequently terrified Western Europe. Interest in foreign affairs is keen. Dramatization of the agrarian, the domestic, and the industrial fronts are not the only theses of the new theatre. A play like Byvoli's *Rubber* plunges into the turmoil of foreign relations and policies. Early in the régime Tretiakov wrote the more important *Roar China,* in which the playwright challenged the exploitation of the Orient by the Imperialistic powers. The play is now a decade old, but the force of its message is very much alive today. In the earlier period the theatre was more concerned with world revolution and the auditoriums more frequently resounded with plays like Ehrenburg's *Destruction of Europe* and Bill-Belotserkovski's incitive *Echo,* but revolution by achievement and example has supplanted, to a degree, the spread of faith by the sword. Imaginary plays on the failure of capitalism are no longer a necessity when a realistic battle is now being fought in Europe. When Soviet fliers landed on the American Pacific coast, the mileage between San Francisco and Moscow shrank by the thousand miles.

Within the year, Afinogenov's *Hail Spain* was written to meet the popular demand. Shostakovitch composed the incidental music. The Maly Theatre gave the première after half a month of rehearsals—record time for the Union, where it is usual to consume a year in preparing a play for the opening night. *Hail Spain* is a journalistic report of the unfortunate Spanish Civil War. The sympathies of the author are naturally on the side of the Government forces. In ten very melodramatic scenes the story of bloody rebellion unfolds. The play senses a likeness between this present Revolution and the days of Red and White struggles in the Union. The Loyalist forces are unprepared and undisciplined; the Rebels are provisioned, organized, and trained. The drama, in true Soviet fashion, ends not with a pessimistic cry of despair but with a shout of victory and triumph. "Let us die upon our feet, rather than live upon our knees," is the defiant battle song of the play. Afinogenov has had examples aplenty for the writing of this drama of civil strife.

In *Hail Spain* Afinogenov must stretch his imagination to create an optimistic ending. There was nothing hypothetical, however, about the last act of Vodopianov's *The Dream,* although coincidence aided the playwright to spell more surely than he knew. For several years the Arctic has been the source of lively interest to the Soviet Government. There is more than abstract scientific satisfaction in conquering the endless ice fields and establishing trade routes across the brink of silence. The north passage for shipping had been opened, but to conquer the polar regions by air remained until 1937 a distant dream.

The Dream invents the story of an aviator, Bezfamilny, who willed to cross the Arctic wastes. Misfortune and illness interrupt his plans. The expedition is given into the hands of others, who carry out the mission badly and are forced down on the ice-floes. The whole band is believed lost. The hero of the play, having recovered, pilots the relief plane not only to the help of the unfortunate aviators but to the successful completion of the mission. "The task of the government is fulfilled. The North Pole is ours." More thrilling than the play itself is the dramatic coincidence that the day of the première in Moscow the author realized his dream in fact and planted the Soviet flag upon the northernmost point of the earth.

The Dream, Roar China, and *Hail Spain* are examples only of a great mass of theatre literature which concerns itself with the broader interests of the Soviet State. These plays of world concern are not viewed with delight by foreign powers. Building a dam in the Volga basin has little to do with the nations in session at Geneva. *Roar China* may be considered a challenge. The standard of good drama, however, does not demand that the thesis of the play must be accepted, but the handling of the thesis must be such that the play appears credible to those who are unfamiliar with the local conditions, problems, and philosophies which it expresses. When the playwrights of the Soviet Union write for a universal theatre, it is only fair to expect them to speak in a language which is not too provincial.

Two universal themes have received very provincial treatment in the new theatre. Liquor and religion have furnished playwrights with an abundance of material of questionable value. Both subjects are looked upon according to Soviet ideology as anesthetics which enable the user to escape from a realist's world. Prohibition was tried in the Union and, as in the United States, failed. The Great Russians know something about the abuse of alcohol and are convinced that it does not mix with increased tempos and efficiencies, but it is hard to make rapid progress against the demon rum. The theatre makes half-hearted attempts to lend its services to the cause of temperance, but the plays are about as effectual as *The Drunkard* and *Ten Nights in a Bar-room,* which American audiences now find quaintly amusing.

The war against religion is a more controversial matter. The Soviet Union permits absolute freedom of belief, but the Government holds the constitutional right to teach agnosticism. The new theatre becomes a natural schoolroom for anti-Christian and, for that matter, anti-spiritual teaching and anti-mystical doctrine or philosophy in general. These plays, written principally to counter the influence of the Greek Church and break down those superstitions with which the new government felt the Synod enchained the ignorant, thereby defeating education and progress, have run the usual gamut of all Soviet propaganda pieces. Violent at first, they mellowed as the conversion of the people to Communistic standards grew. Today the force of the original onslaught against religion is preserved principally in divorced scenes and incidental situations only. Entire plays are not often devoted to the war on the faiths.

In a play like *The Wandering School* the traditional classroom prayer is enacted as a stupid, empty form which youngsters meaninglessly mouth with little sense of inner grace. In *Resurrection,* the swearing-in of witnesses before the high tribunal is done with fulsome elaboration and minute, vulgar attention to kissing the book. In *Carmen* the Toreadors cross themselves extravagantly before risking their lives in the bullring. Wherever the opportunity is offered, ridicule and burlesque of bell and book lurk behind direction and acting. Even in serious dramatic moments, any formal ritualistic devotion is played sardonically with tongue in cheek. The laughter and snickering of the audience at such moments indicate that the theatre has found a new, if temporary, source of comedy. The stranger, if he is tolerant, will not let this anti-religious demonstration spoil his evening in the playhouse. Plays written with complete disrespect for religion are bound to see social relationships in a very different perspective from that accepted by the Western World.

Religion, marriage, labor on farm and in factory, friendships, loyalties, intimate sentiments—all have undergone a metamorphosis. The new theatre reflects the times and attempts to be the brief chronicle of the moment. Is it any wonder that the plays are foreign to the experience of those trained in another philosophy? Ivan Babichev in *A Conspiracy of Feelings* is sincerely muddled by the confusion of it all. "People must stop loving each other. There will be no more traitors, no brave men, no true friends." The new theatre answers that the old emotions have not been lost; that they are being directed into deeper channels; that they are, for the first time, becoming useful in building a new world. The Kremlin bells continue to clang out the quarter hours, but the Basilica of St. Basil is sadly in need of repair.

THE THEATRE IN THE PROVINCES

VIII

The Theatre in the Provinces

AMERICA HAS BEEN called "the melting pot." For half a century this country well deserved that title, but first honors in the difficult process of amalgamation are now the possession of the Soviet Union. A tabulation of the population of the U. S. S. R. presents a cloak as varied in colors as Joseph's. Great Russians, Ukrainians, Georgians, Tartars, Turcomanians, Armenians, Uzbeks, White Russians, Jews, Finns, and Mongolians are but a few of those who complicate the racial picture with a Bedlam of tongues. To build a secure proletarian culture for all these races is a colossal undertaking which staggers the imagination.

The policy under the Imperial Russian eagles was the complete suppression and, in some cases, the annihilation of the national minorities. A belligerent program, known as Russification, to superimpose the Great Russian tongue and culture upon all, was rigorously pursued. The practice was inaugurated with the theoretic platform that in one language there is unity and in unity there is strength. The Tzarist régime believed it just and reasonable to employ the military in carrying through this leveling process. Culture was reduced to the common denominator of the Slavophil tradition, and speech was curbed to conform to the accent of Leningrad and Moscow.

In the eyes of the Revolutionary Government this policy appeared futile and brutal. The Soviet Party substituted for the old plan a scheme wherein the racial traditions of each people should be respected and the right of self-determination of the various nationalities should be maintained. The free development of ethnographic groups was encouraged. To carry out this program, it has been necessary in special cases to create grammars— even alphabets—for those tribal languages which existed only in oral form. Newspapers, schools, and theatres are now conducted in the speech of the particular minority. Language as the centralizing force has been replaced by the ideology of the communistic faith.

In such a scheme the Soviet theatre has had a significant work to do. The severely high artistic standards which have been developed in the central playhouses of Moscow and Leningrad have been set up as guide-

posts for the Georgian, the Ukrainian, and the Tartar. The classical repertories have been revamped and restaged to fit the emotional understanding
of each people. An example of this principle of adaptation was seen recently
in New York. *Macbeth* was produced in Harlem, not as a Scotsman's
story but as an African tribal drama. Some felt that a Dunsinane made of
bamboo was too absurd. Yet Broadway reset *Prénèz garde à la peinture*
on a New England farm and changed the French provincials to Swamp
Yankees. The producer felt that America would enjoy and understand the
play better in a Massachusetts milieu, and America did. To adapt the play
to suit the emotional receptivity of the particular audience is the principle
which theatres of the national minorities apply to the standard drama.

The classics, as in the great centers, supply only a part of the repertory.
Creative work is emphasized. There was Stenka Razin in the Great Russias;
in Georgia there was Arsen. The Rustaveli Theatre has its own play to
parallel the Robin Hood of the Moscow scene. *The Armored Train*
becomes *Anzor* in Tiflis. Folksongs and countryside legends are retold in
theatre scenarios. The dances and ballads become colorful material for the
nationalistic ballet and opera. Naturally, love of spectacle and pageantry
can be overdone. The primitive peoples are overfond of action and display.
There is always a possibility that national groups, enthusiastically sub-
merging themselves in their rich provincial resources, can lose sight of
responsibility to the Union proper and slip into the error of decentraliza-
tion. The new theatre—letting well enough alone—finds such an obstacle
of slight importance, however, if creative work is checked only by adherence
to high artistic ideals.

The progress of some of these nationalistic groups has already attracted
international attention. The Jewish Theatre in Moscow has been extravagantly praised by visitors, particularly from America. Granovski and
Vakhtangov both were associated with its fortunes in earlier days. Some
of the plays in its repertory have become standard drama. Broadway has
seen Aleikhem's *Two Hundred Thousand.* Bergelson is now recognized
as an established playwright with *The Deaf One* and *The Measure of
Severity* to his credit. *The Three Ravens, At Night, The Travels of
Benjamin III,* Goldfaden's *Shulamite* and *The Witch,* Mizandrontsev's
The Wailing Wall, and Babel's *Decadence* form but an introduction to
the wealth of the repertory which this theatre presents with an abandoned
vim and vigor. Its acting, its settings, its plays mirror truthfully the deeper
artistic resources of the Hebrew people. Its work is generally admired,
and its standards and methods have been reflected in Jewish theatres
throughout the world.

Closely associated with the Jewish National is the Gypsy Theatre. The reason for this friendly connection is not far to seek, for Goldblat, the director, and Tishev, the designer, have both given much attention to this youthful national minority enterprise which plays half its season in competition with the Moscow playhouses and the remainder in camps and villages throughout the Union. The plays are performed in the Romany tongue and the repertory is in the main the work of Gypsy playwrights. Starting in 1931 with exhibitions of songs and descriptive dances, the strength of the company reached a high-tide mark after three years in a distinguished adaptation of *Carmen*. This is not the Bizet opera but a brand new play with music. The atmosphere of Spain a century ago is recaptured in a text which lends Carmen the character of an abused nomadic maiden and which is supplemented by a score based on Spanish Gypsy songs. The composer is Bugatchevsky.

The principal dramatist of the group is Guermano, who wrote for this theatre its first play, *Life On Wheels,* a loosely constructed piece, interlaced with music, which explains the fall of tribal autocracy and the establishment of the wanderers as settled farmers. A second play by the same author, *Between Two Fires,* carries the spectator back to the Civil War and explains that the Gypsy chiefs favored the aristocrats but the tribe generally favored the Red Army. Victory once more comes to the masses who cast their lot with the forces of the Revolution. *Pharoah's Tribe,* written by the Russian Svertchkov, is also a war play, but represents the struggle of 1914 and not that of the Civil War. The plot describes the suffering which the great conflict caused the Hungarian Gypsy tribes. Of more recent date are two plays, *The Camp in the Steppes* and *The Gypsies.* The latter derives its plot from a poem by Pushkin. Like the wandering people from whom these talented actors descended, the Gypsy National Theatre is itself a nomadic enterprise. Since the Gypsies are scattered along the highways and byways of the Union, the Romany audience for these players is not found in a single locality but is encamped everywhere along the open road. Though Moscow is the central stand, the Gypsies truly have a theatre on wheels.

One of the oldest and most important minority theatres is the Georgian Rustaveli, whose home stage in Tiflis has echoed to the native music of Polishvilli and the fiery tirades of Chanchachvili. There were futile efforts made to establish a state theatre in Georgia before the Revolution, but success was pathetically slight because of the imperial policy of Russification. In Civil War days an ambitious group organized the first really native theatre, which came under the direction of Akhmetelli in 1925. This headstrong and thoroughly competent *regisseur* soon proved his worth by a production of Rabakedze's *Lamara,* which spins a romance of feuds and elemental love among the mountain tribesmen.

Akhmetelli has repeatedly exhibited his rare power. He has a talent for seeing equally well the world or local events lighted by the clear and stimulating sunshine of his native crags and notches. The Russian *Armored Train* actually becomes a different play in Tiflis; Schiller's *Robbers* loses its nineteenth century stupidities and is fired by a credible contemporary spark when staged among the Georgian hills. Akhmetelli not only produces but also stimulates playwrights and composers to create in the elusive mood of his theatre. Dadiani's *Tetnuld*—an intense drama of the passing of the patriarchal religion before the advances of science— nestles among the local peaks and breathes forth a depth of feeling that has won for it in the Soviet Union the interesting title of "first Soviet tragedy." Dadiani has recently written another most successful play, *From a Spark.* Arsen, likewise, illustrates the infectious enthusiasm which Akhmetelli seems able to transfer to the writers.

Chanchachvili, the author of *Arsen,* could well be called the leading Georgian playwright. It was he who derived the text of *Anzor* from Ivanov's *Armored Train.* His latest work is *1905,* which brings to the stage some episodes from the youth of Comrade Stalin. *Arsen* is a success- ful attempt to write for the Rustaveli its own epic drama and to parallel the Russian *Stenka Razin.* The hero, for whom the play is named, is a clansman leading a revolt in the last century against the imperial soldiers and the government henchmen. This shepherd general typifies the moun- taineers' love for freedom and personifies the spirit which in 1917 established this minority state as an independent republic. The sacking of an overlord's castle, the defense of a mountain pass, the thwarted treachery of a jealous peasant, the stoically heroic parting of Arsen's condemned younger brother from his mother are a few of the scenes which sweep with the roar of a mountain stream before a background of massive grandeur and unusual beauty.

The Georgian Theatre has shown a peculiar aptitude for creating majestic settings, for manipulating ungainly masses of players into balanced and graceful ensembles, for giving all movement a liquid rhythm that hauntingly suggests the native dances. The stage pictures are traditionally magnificent. With a strange magic this theatre has dramatized the blue sky, the sturdy mountains, and the broad grazing lands into a new type of virile romantic drama which speaks in bold, melodramatic accents to the glorification of Georgia and the Soviet Minority Theatres.

Though the Rustaveli is the principal state theatre of Georgia, it is forced to share honors with the Mardzhanov in Tiflis and with nearly twenty-five other enterprising units scattered throughout the Republic. Of almost equal importance with this very advanced minority state theatre is the ambitious program of the Ukraine, whose central theatre is at Karkov. For this group Korneichuk wrote his prize drama *The Last of the Squadron.* Semikov's *The Wedding,* a collective farm play, has been seen in Leningrad as well as on native soil. Composers like Uanovski and Zolataryev are busily at work. In 1937 *Shchors,* a local opera, was sung at the twentieth anniversary celebration. The Ukrainian Jewish Theatre emulates its Moscow elder, tries to surpass its sister group at Minsk, and boasts its Reznik. Some Ukrainians dream of the day when their national minority theatres may make the parent stages in Great Russia fight to hold first place. The enthusiasm should be commended even though one smiles.

Both the Ukrainian and the Georgian state enterprises owe their leading position among the minorities to the fact that Tiflis and Karkov were not without a tradition for plays and opera before the establishment of the new national policy. The younger theatres, which have developed without the benefit of older tradition, need not, however, bow their heads in shame. The Armenian group is very ambitious in opera and drama. Djanan, an actor in the company at the State Dramatic Theatre at Erivan, has had the honor to see his play *Shah-Name* produced. From the Turcoman Theatre at Ashkabad comes news of an oriental romance entitled *In the Sands of Kara-Kum.* Baku is playing *Othello,* and *Hamlet* is popular with the Uzbeks. What these lesser groups are playing is for the moment, however, not nearly so important as the thought that the far corners, which it has pleased the Western World to think beyond the civilized pale, at last have theatres of their own. In one of these corners of the forgotten hinterlands is a country, almost unheard of in America, which is making impressive strides in theatre art.

Stretching along the shores of the Caspian Sea is the Republic of Kazakstan, comprising a territory almost as great as Central Europe. At the time of the Revolution ninety percent of the natives were illiterate. The Tzarist order had stultified, sometimes through brutal force, the development of Kazak art and music. When the release came, the pent-up creative instincts of the people surged to the fore and naturally found expression in the drama. The theatre of Kazakstan is in every sense a new theatre, yet the traditions from which it has grown are as old as the dawn of Western civilization.

In less than a decade the Kazak stage has become an important part of the Soviet system. Shakspere is not too heavy nor Katayev too light for this occidental-oriental people. In 1936 the State Theatre of Kazakstan was called to Moscow and there presented several of its original plays. *Zhablyv* is a historical revolutionary piece, built by the measure of *Stenka Razin* and *Arsen,* in which the revolt of Kazaks against the Imperial Government the year before the overthrow of Tzardom is glorified. Less a made-to-order play is *Kyz-Zhibek,* a romance of the Dark Ages adapted from folklore by the national playwright Mussepov. Ballet, naturally abetted by the instinctive feeling of the Kazak for dancing, is growing in popularity. Native opera is sure to follow.

The Kazak drama is very elemental. To the more sophisticated it might appear naïve. The popular love for singing and dancing leads the Kazaks to interpolate these elements into the plays at the slightest provocation. It is as yet impossible for them to formulate a clear distinction between musical and dramatic plays. At present they are learning to express themselves, and they are making a progress which is astonishing and a credit to the policy of the new theatre.

The Theatre of the Soviet Union is daily lengthening the radius of its influence. Fresh themes, fresh ideas, fresh theatrical methods are bound to come from the hitherto uncultivated sources of atmosphere and temperament among the National Minorities. As time passes, it is more than likely that significant contributions will be made not only to the dramatic art of the Union but to the world as well. Proletarian Culture encourages the development of nationalistic cultures. The Theatre of the People does not measure its borders by the city limits of Moscow. The Mongolians, Finns, and Tartars are also being taught to say "OUR THEATRE." There is still a Bedlam of tongues, but the mighty chorus is learning to speak with one thought.

WHEAT FROM CHAFF

IX

Wheat From Chaff

N EVALUATION of the *Theatre at the Left,* unless guided by the judgment of Solomon, can at best be little more than a series of personal opinions reflecting a rutted and precon-ceived notion of what the drama ought to be. To sift the wheat from the chaff presents further difficulties in that before a critical ray has passed the lens of observation, the design of colored glass has shifted into a fresh kaleidoscopic formation. Mutability can be strength, for static theatre easily deteriorates into decadent theatre, but feverish experiment permits no form to crystalize. Some phases of this new theatre can be noted, however, with moderate surety.

The reality of a *Theatre at the Left* is not an ephemeral dream. In 1927 there may have been reasonable doubt that a drama parented by Marxian philosophy might ever experience a permanent existence on the stage. In 1938 the new theatre is an established fact. The Union has demonstrated to the most incredulous that a mass theatre with a cultural purpose can be operated successfully under governmental subsidy; that a non-commercial theatre, the hope of artists the world over, actually exists. The enthusiastic pioneers of 1917 are growing old. A group of fledgling playwrights, designers, and actors, creating for an audience which does not have to be trained out of its bourgeois attitudes, are, in this twentieth anniversary year, the leaders. The new theatre was projected by the Meyerholds; the established theatre of the U. S. S. R. is the theatre of the Okhpoklovs, the Simonovs, the Akimovs. A new generation born after the Revolution now controls this weapon for building proletarian culture. The *Theatre at the Left* has reached a healthy majority.

The busy, youthful leaders are inclined to believe that they have created the best theatre in the world. Too many foreign visitors are swept off their feet into the rapid, flood current of the Union's self-adulation and believe as ardently as do the sons of the sickle and hammer. The *Theatre at the Left* is not, however, the best theatre in the world. Maybe there is no *best* theatre, but surely the theatres of London, of Berlin, of Paris, of New York are no skeletons in armor to fool the public. There are still able designers, progressive playwrights, honest artistic actors, and brilliant ingenious directors to be found working on Broadway, and some of them work in a very quiet, modest fashion. No, the *Theatre at the Left* is not the last word in excellence; but Moscow has made a beginning, and in another twenty years may justly boast the first theatre in the world as the achievement. At present, that this is the most progressive theatre is difficult to deny.

Progressiveness is obtrusively apparent in Soviet stagecraft, which already has left more than fingerprints upon Continental and American settings. There is hardly a possible mode of expression which the new theatre has failed to try. The conventional is the exception rather than the rule, though this does not mean that the weird and bizarre have scattered all other forms before them. There is a perceptible trend in design away from the theories of the cubist and constructivist toward those of the illusionist, but pure naturalism is not especially admired, nor are those baffling extravagances current at the Kamerny or the Meyerhold theatres a decade ago. The work of Nikolai Akimov is proof of sanely directed energy and confident power in creation; many hail him chief of the artist-producer-designers. A multitude of other young men can legitimately claim distinguished recognition. Rindin, Rabinovich, Tishler, Williams, and Nivinsky are established; new and gifted names press to the fore each season.

Due to labor and material differences in production cost, the elaborate-ness and massiveness of the settings which these designers create take away the breath of those accustomed to the London and New York theatres. Hillsides, open ocean, mountain roads, crystal palaces, and forest glades, which demand platform construction too vast for the proscenium arch of most American theatres, are child's play for the technicians of Moscow and Leningrad. The magnificence of costumes and properties matches the intricate and elaborate spectacle provided by the appropriate backgrounds. In contrast to these expressions of opulence, the generally inadequate and sometimes naïve lighting is a shocking blemish.

All this emphasis upon setting does not overshadow or diminish the importance of the central artist of the theatre through whom plays have their being. The actor ever holds the center stage in the *Theatre at the Left*. Visitors have with one voice been loud in their praise of Soviet acting. Training these thespians have had; their studied technique pro-claims how competent they are in handling the tools of their trade. Their ensemble playing might be justly envied by any theatrical company outside the Union. But even though the group acting is superior, the individual performances seldom exhibit the compelling power which is generally accredited them. Praise is surely due to artists like Glizer, Shchukin, Kuhnen, Dobroliubov, Kachalov, Simonov, and their many able comrade colleagues. Such praise should not imply that Cornell, Gielgud, Hayes, Jouvet, and Evans do not exist. All of the great actors have not been herded into the theatre of the Soviet Union. "There is a world elsewhere." Genius is not particular whether it is born in a capitalistic cradle or in a communistic manger.

Actors, producers, and designers are all dependent upon a text. The playwright cannot be neglected in theatrical enterprises. On more than one occasion Tairov has implied that the weakness of the *Theatre at the Left* is the dearth of able writers for the stage. There have been foreign visitors who have gone so far as to report that the Soviet Union has as yet produced no dramatists. This is an overharsh criticism; but severe though it may be, it is not without foundation. Obvious faults in these craftsmen flaunt themselves in the new theatre. Playwrights are self-consciously circumscribed by the strictures of the collective philosophy; characterizations slump into types and caricatures; structure is generally inefficient.

Censorship, pushed at times to absurd lengths by the powerful extremists, without a doubt has mercilessly cowed the playwrights into a corner where they are bound to lose the drama for the politics. In the earlier days there was ample reason for the new theatre to carry the faith to the people, like Mahomet with sword in hand. To convert a nation wholesale trans-forms art into a weapon which might be mistaken for a mediæval battle-axe. Granting the necessity for noisy propaganda in times of stress, such an epoch is passed now. Could not the playwrights learn to be true to the spirit of Marx without constantly blatting politics or bemiring themselves on the domestic or agrarian front? Surely plays can be written in harmony with the industrialization of a nation and the dictatorship of the proletariat without wearing a political chip ostentatiously on the shoulder. The material of the playwright has been swamped by an overload of ideology; the characters which bear the burden of plot have also suffered through overzealous adherence to doctrine.

Mass individuals are easily created for a mass drama. Types are more easily created than true human beings. In the valiant struggle to subordinate the individual to the group, abstraction slides unhindered into the place of personality. Gorki, master creator of real, breathing characters, saw this danger in the new playwrights and pointed it out to them before he died. Poster writing finds black and white characters adequate, but the world is still filled with the grey. If the Soviet playwright is honestly searching for truth, he might well remember that although his ideal remains the man for the mass, the individual in any civilization still retains a personality. The greatest of the writers for the theatre of social relation-ships knew this. No harm would come to the younger craftsmen through a study of the dramaturgy of the Playwright of the Masses and the Artist of the People.

Too much ideology may have held the material and the characterization of the Soviet playwright in rigid check, but Marxian theories can hardly be held responsible for the carelessness of the play structure which is often representative of nothing short of slovenly workmanship. Selection is a primary quality of any art. Aesthetics devised on a sociological-economic plan cannot change this axiom. To string together disjointed incidents like so many beads on a string is one way to foster the creation of tedious plays. The Soviet playwright can pick the scene which teems with theatrical power. Frequently he obscures such a scene in an arid waste of unim-portant detail. Gorki and Ostrovski were not masters of plot, but they more than made up for this deficiency through expert portrayal of charac-ter. Perhaps the younger Soviet dramatists have copied the outward faults of two great leaders in the old Russian theatre and have failed to imitate their virtues. Many of Shakspere's imitators did just this; the record of their folly is spread over the first fifty years of the nineteenth century.

The contentious Soviet playwright would likely defend himself against this challenge by saying that it was not his classical models but malice aforethought which led him astray in escaping from the banal conventions of the well-made play which had stultified Continental and American authors from 1900 to the World War. The more charitable critics at home and abroad might suggest that extreme youth and unbridled enthusiasm would be reasonable explanations. A multitude of ideas and emotions can confuse when the playwright burns to say everything at once. Whatever may or may not be the sources of the fault, according to the standards of the Western theatre world, for which the Union has little regard, the dramaturgy of the *Theatre at the Left* walks on crutches. Many of the younger writers recognize their shortcomings. Surely, powerful, well constructed texts will soon appear on the stage. The new theatre is ever anxious to improve. It will not let this handicap continue unheeded.

In this new theatre designers, actors, producers, playwrights, and audiences are all working together. Their solidarity is an ever present strength for meeting and surmounting obstacles. Today all dramatic crafts are discussing synthesis. The ambition is to concentrate energies in a single method, to relate all experimentation in a common artistic scheme, and to discover an indisputable formula for proletarian culture. The new theatre is optimistic, spontaneous, vital. It is a theatre for the strong, and revels in its realism. It is confident, unafraid of constructive criticism, progressive. It is a theatre of action which has no place for escapist creators or passive receivers.

Above all, the new theatre has charted its course. Pogodin closes his play *My Friend* with the thought that they know what they want, and that is to create a secure, happy, classless society. The Soviet theatre is devoted to this ideal. Education and artistic creation move forward hand in hand with industrialization. When you know where you are going it is not too difficult to get there. The new theatre knows its goal and is determined. In twenty years it has compelled the theatrical eyes of the world to look toward the Kremlin walls. The day is not yet, but the American and European scene had best train for the race if advantage is to be held against the youthful pace of the *Theatre at the Left*.

EXPLANATIONS

Meyerhold has been retired from office. Reasons suggested for this action are that he was too autocratic in the management of his theatre and that his vague theories were not easily understood by the masses. This change may bring Tairov and Okhlopkov to first rank as leaders of the "inwardist school." Such a thought is confirmed by the amalgamation of the Kamerny and Realistic Theatres.

Kirschon and Afinogenov are in difficulties with the Government. In the theatre, as elsewhere in the U. S. S. R., men of prominence and promise seem to live in the shadow. That they are sometimes returned to favor is witnessed in the fact that Shostakovitch has risen to the fore again through his *Fifth Symphony* (1938).

Seats are not free and prices are not low in the Soviet Theatre. "How can the public afford to attend?" The answer lies in the fact that theatre is not an entertaining luxury, but a cultural force in the U. S. S. R. No one is forced to attend, however.

Pravda (truth) and *Izvestia* are powerful newspapers in Moscow. Naturally, they are under governmental control, for the Soviet Republic is a Communist State. Both these journals pride themselves on their dramatic criticisms. Markov has been dramatic critic for both.

The Theatre of the National Minorities because of its extent and mushroom growth has not been thoroughly studied. The reports of yesterday are stale indeed before they can be recorded. *The Theatre Arts Monthly* has published articles of merit on the Gypsy Theatre (Lozowick, April 1936), the Turcoman Theatre (Lozowick, November 1933), the Rustaveli Theatre (Leyda, January 1936), and the Theatrical Olympiad (Strong, December 1930). *Soviet Russia Today* has interesting news of the minorities in almost every issue. *Kazak Art* (September 1937) was well discussed by Altaisky.

The Research Bulletin of the Soviet Union, published semi-monthly by the American Russian Institute, is always filled with authentic theatre and musical notes. *The Development of Soviet Music* (April 30, 1937) by Nicholas Slonimsky is an excellent analysis of the growth of music for the masses.

The Theatre Arts Monthly published its September issue in 1936 under the title, *The Soviet Theatre Speaks for Itself*. This number includes articles by Kirschon, Markov, Meyerhold, and Akimov. There is also a well selected bibliography on the Soviet Theatre.

The amateur theatre is very active. There are numerous workers' theatres, farm collective theatres, and children's and adult's dramatic clubs. Some of these, as in America, attain a proficiency which is almost professional.

The temperamental character of the Slav partly explains the need for extravagantly protracted rehearsal periods in the Soviet Theatre. Do the results warrant the expenditure of time? There are those who believe that the New York Theatre Guild and many of McClintic's productions accomplish as satisfactory results in six weeks as does the Vakhtangov of Moscow after a year of preparation. Hurried production can result in carelessness, but fuddling about does not spell perfection.

Norris Houghton's *Moscow Rehearsals* is a fine analysis of Soviet production and acting. He speaks with authority. Further than that *Moscow Rehearsals* is direct and clear.

Huntley Carter's books are inclusive records of the first ten years of the new theatre.

The summary article by Mr. Henry Dana on the Soviet Theatre in Dickinson's *Theatre in a Changing Europe* presents a graphic picture of the new utilitarian drama. His new comprehensive bibliography is a definitive record of the plays and movements from 1917 to 1938. This volume will represent two decades of first-hand work in the field. It is to be published by the American-Russian Institute.

Markov's *Soviet Theatre*, known better in England than in America, presents the drama from the Soviet point of view. The exposition of the new ideology is particularly worthwhile.

The Rustaveli Theatre is named in memory of the twelfth century Georgian poet, Shota Rustaveli, who is remembered today for his epic, *The Knight in the Tiger Skin*.

REFERENCES

The following books have been used as references in the
preparation of the THEATRE AT THE LEFT.

GENERAL

Arkhangelsky, A., *Leningrad*..Leningrad Soviet Press
Bable, Tolstoy, and Others, *Azure Cities*................................International Publishers
Block, A. L., *A Pocket Guide to the Soviet Union*.........................Vneshtorgisdat
Brown, W. A., *The Groping Giant*...Yale Press
Callcott, M. S., *Russian Justice*...Macmillan
Chamberlain, W. H., *Collectivism: A False Utopia*............................Macmillan
Chamberlin, W. H., *Soviet Russia*..Little, Brown
Citrine, W., *I Search For Truth in Russia*..Dutton
Coates, W. P. and Z. K., *Scenes From Soviet Life*.............International Publishers
Duranty, W., *I Write As I Please*..Simon, Schuster
Fadeyev, A., *The Nineteen*..International Publishers
Farson, N., *The Way of a Transgressor*...............................Harcourt, Brace
Freeman, J., *The Soviet Worker*.................................International Publishers
Gantt, W. H., *Russian Medicine*...Hoeler
Gladkov, F., *Cement*..International Publishers
Glaeser and Weiskopf, *The Land Without Unemployment*, International Publishers
Gide, A., *Return From the U. S. S. R.*..Knopf

HISTORY

Gorky, M., *On Guard For the Soviet Union*......................International Publishers
Hindus, M., *Moscow Skies*..Random House
Lyons, E., *We Cover the World*...Harcourt, Brace
Malevsky-Malevitch, P., *The Soviet Union Today*...Paisley
Nodel, W. A., *Supply and Trade in the U. S. S. R.*...........................Gollancz
Nurina, F., *Women in the Soviet Union*.........................International Publishers
Pinkevich, H. P., *Science and Education in the U. S. S. R.*.....................Gollancz
Strong, A. L., *The Soviet World*...Holt
Semashko, N. A., *Health Protection in the U. S. S. R.*.........................Gollancz
Williams, A. R., *The Soviets*...Harcourt, Brace
Yason, J. D., *Foreign Trade in the U. S. S. R.*....................................Gollancz
Gorky, M., *Days With Lenin*.....................................International Publishers
Hindus, M., *Humanity Uprooted*..Cape and Smith
Marx, K., *Capital*..The Modern Library
Platonov, S. F., *A History of Russia*...Macmillan
Reed, J., *Ten Days that Shook the World*.......................International Publishers
Ruhle, O., *Karl Marx*..Star
Serge, V., *From Lenin to Stalin*..Pioneer
Strong, A. L., *The New Soviet Constitution*..Holt
Trotsky, L., *Literature and Revolution*..........................International Publishers
Trotsky, L., *The History of the Russian Revolution*....................Simon, Schuster
Walsh, E. A., *The Fall of the Russian Empire*................................Blue Ribbon

THEATRES AND ARTS

Baksley, A., *The Path of the Modern Russian Stage*................Palmer and Hayward

Brown, J. M., *The Modern Theatre in Revolt*................Norton

Bulletin of the Soviet Union, *Files to vol. III, No. 2*.........Russian American Institute

Carter, H., *The New Spirit in the European Theatre*................Doran

Carter, H., *The New Spirit in the Russian Theatre*................Shaylor

Carter, H., *The New Theatre and Cinema in Soviet Russia*................Chapman, Dodd

Cherniavsky, L. M., Editor, *The Moscow Theatre for Children*.........Iskra Revolutsii

Deutsch and Yarmolinsky, *Russian Poetry*................International Publishers

Deyawin, C., *Hundert Jahre des Staatlichen Dramatischen Theatres*......Staatsverlag

Dickenson, T. H., *The Theatre in a Changing Europe*................Holt

Eastman, M., *Art and Literature in the Soviet Union*................Paisley

Evreinoff, N., *The Chief Thing*................Doubleday, Page

Freeman, Kunitz and Lozowick, *Voices of October*................Vanguard

Gogol, N., *The Inspector General* (introduction)................Knopf

Gogol, N., *The Gamblers* (introduction)................Macaulay

Gregor and Fulop-Miller, *The Russian Theatre*................Lippincott

Houghton, N., *Moscow Rehearsals*................Harcourt, Brace

Ivanov, V., *Armoured Train* (foreword)................International Publishers

Lyons, E., *Six Soviet Plays* (introductions)................Houghton, Mifflin

Kirchon and Ouspensky, *Red Rust*................Brentano's

Leningrad, *History of the Soviet Theatre*................U. S. S. R. State Press

Magnus and Walter, *Three Plays of Lunacharski*................Routledge

Markov, P. A., *The Soviet Theatre*................Gollancz

Meyerhold, V., *On Theatre*................Moscow

Moscow Art Theatre, *Series of Russian Plays*................Brentano's

Moscow, *The Theatres of Moscow*................Vneshtorgisdat

Moscow, *Programs, Announcements, etc.*................Printed for Intourist

Nemirovitch-Dantchenko, *My Life in the Russian Theatre*................Little, Brown

Noyes, G. R., *Plays by Alexander Ostrovsky* (introduction)................Scribners

Olgin, M. J., *Maxim Gorky*................International Publishers

Sabaneyeff, L., *Modern Russian Composers*................International Publishers

Sayler, O. M., *The Russian Theatre*................Brentano's

Schwezoff, I., *Russian Somersault*................Harper's

Simonson, L., *The Stage Is Set*................Harcourt, Brace

Smith, J., Editor, *Soviet Russia Today*................Complete Files to January 1938

Stanislavsky, C., *My Life In Art*................Little, Brown

Stanislavsky, C., *An Actor Prepares*................Theatre Arts

Tairov, A., *Notes of a Regisseur*................Moscow

Theatre Arts Monthly, *Files 1924-1937 Complete*................

Tretiakov, S. *Roar China* (foreword)................International Publishers

Wiener, L., *The Contemporary Drama of Russia*................Little, Brown

An attempt has been made, not too happily in some cases, to transcribe proper names in a simple form which a general reader will not find too confusing. The Slavic languages employ many letters and symbols which have no ready English equivalent.